V⭐ICE⭐VER ACHIEVER

Brand Your VO Career.
Change Your Life.

By Celia Siegel

ISBN-13: 978-0692991800

ISBN-10: 0692991808

For my mother, Alberta, who taught me
to see what is special in everyone.

CONTENTS

ACKNOWLEDGMENTS

So glad you picked up this book! I wrote it because I want to take you on a journey to discover the wonderful brand that resides within you. I believe that all voice talent deserve a brand and the confidence and attention that come with it. I know from first-hand experience how having an authentic personal brand can elevate your career and change your life. Don't believe me? I dare you to try it.

I could not have written this book without the help of my multi-awesome editor, Heidi Raschke, who would not let me use the word "multi-awesome" in this book. Thanks also to my longtime friend and brand writer extraordinaire, Marnie Lee, my smart, tactical marketing manager, Amber Kinney, and my fearless sales strategist, Martha Kahn. Thanks also to Biondo Studio for their spot-on design work on this and many creative projects throughout the years. They all helped me get this book into your hands. Last but not least, thanks to the superstar voice talent community who make it possible for me to have the coolest job in the world.

Chop, chop, lollipop! Let's go discover your one-of-a-kind personal brand!

CHAPTER 1:

CHOOSING TO KILL IT IN THE NEW VOICEOVER WORLD

Make the disruption in our industry work for you

Congratulations — you're in one of the most amazing industries in the world! And my apologies — you're also in one of the most insanely competitive industries in the world.

Once upon a time in a land not so far away, a person could get ahead in the voiceover business with a solid resume. Agents and clients wanted to know: Where have you worked and what have you done?

There was a sense of business proof. The thinking went: "If she's good enough for Coke and Yoplait, certainly she'll make me look good." But times have changed.

At the 2016 SOVAS voiceover convention, which took place in Los Angeles that year, one of the top agents in the country, Ken Slevin of CESD, took questions from the stage after accepting the Backstage Vanguard Award. One of them was, "With so many submissions each day, how do you decide who to take a chance on and represent?" (And never forget that agents are taking a chance. They work on 100 percent commission. If you don't work, they don't get paid either.)

Slevin's answer:

"Are they **brandable?**"

When I first began working in this industry 28 years ago, all of the talent was booked — 9 a.m., 10 a.m., 11 a.m. – every hour, all day. It was like an ensemble cast of voiceover talent that would cruise around town. Each city had a pool of talented people booked solid doing all of the local voiceover work.

Then came the go-go '90s. The economy was robust, and there was plenty of union work for voice actors. Voiceover became the "it career" of the decade. Legendary voiceover talent Don LaFontaine was bringing in a purported $13 million a year. My clients joked about rolling their checks to the bank in wheelbarrows.

Boy, has the landscape shifted. Having a solid voiceover career these days is like getting into Harvard. You're competing globally against the well-trained masses. The truth is there is more skilled voiceover talent out there than ever before. That makes it harder to stand out — and to know where you stand.

You might be talented. You might be connected. You might be hard-working. And yet, there's a good chance you're frustrated. Not securing enough auditions. Not booking enough. Not being heard. You might be relatively new to the industry. Or you might be further along in your career and hitting walls. Maybe you used to be on top of your game but no longer own the position you once did. Agents and bookings have become elusive. You're feeling shut out. Like one person drowning in a sea of millions instead of the standout one-in-a-million talent you truly are.

If you are relatively new to the biz, it is tempting to feel like you missed out on the glory days. If you have been in voiceover for a long time, it's tempting to spend your precious hours reminiscing about the good old days — before the bubble burst in 2008, before the recession, before social media, before technology both burst open the business and drove down rates, making voiceover more competitive than ever.

I am not going to kid you. Finding success in this business is not easy and all things need to come into alignment, but let's look at the flip side of that coin. Sure, there's more competition, but there are also more opportunities. Voiceover today is a $4 billion industry. The shake-up in our industry is igniting new flames of creativity and opening new doors. I believe this is not an ending but the beginning of a true golden age of voiceover work. Here's your chance to grab a piece of that pie.

As a voiceover talent manager, I've been helping top talent advance their careers and achieve their goals for 15 years. I created my company because while working as a West Coast talent agent, I discovered the reason some truly great talent are successful and some aren't. I noticed that many of even the most talented talent were getting lost in the sound crowd and not being heard, let alone hired. Why? They lacked a strong personal brand.

In addition to this discovery, I recognized seven common denominators of voiceover success or, as I prefer to call them, the Seven Voiceover Superpowers: talent, training, commitment, business skills, connections, support, and branding.

I've seen it over and over again. Only by taking that one superpower you were born with — raw talent — and combining it with the other common denominators to voiceover success, can you become the supertalent you were meant to be.

If you're reading this book, chances are you already have the first three. Raw talent, training, and commitment are the ante you need to participate in the voiceover game. The next three — business skills, connections, and support — can be learned or built. All are necessary, but none of them work without a brand.

**1. Talent   2. Training   3. Commitment
4. Business Skills   5. Connections
6. Support   7. Branding**

Why? Because branding is the most magical superpower of all. Without it, your team, your connections, your business skills, even your talent and commitment are like a shiny, beautiful boat without a rudder.

Branding has the uncanny ability to transform not only your voiceover career but your life — to give you the swagger and confidence to be who you truly are and pulverize the competition (while, of course, maintaining your good standing in the voiceover community). When you put branding at the heart of everything you do, you know where you're heading and you can sail through even the choppiest waters.

Powerful brands determine the success of every product (and person) in the marketplace. Voiceover is no different. In this book, I'll give you proven, fruitful voiceover branding strategies that will empower and propel your voiceover career.

I will:

- Share tips on unearthing the authentic brand that already exists within you
- Help you figure out exactly what your brand should look and feel like
- Show how your brand can work hard for you while you are working hard being creative
- Share tips on how to distribute branded content across a variety of platforms
- Show how a bespoke brand will build confidence and reap big results

I will also help you avoid these common branding mistakes:

- A brand that could be any voiceover talent out there
- A brand that does not match you or your voice
- An inconsistent brand identity
- Trying to appease everyone
- Poor visuals and copywriting
- Not fully committing to your brand
- Not knowing who you really are
- Being inauthentic
- Ignoring social media

I'll also share examples from my client list as well as exercises that will help you uncover your personal brand — one that taps into the essence that is uniquely you. Look for these throughout the book under the headings "Voiceover Brands at Work" and "Take Action," respectively.

When you finish reading this book not only will you have the tools to master your voiceover career but also a soaring confidence that will have ripple effects throughout your life.

Are you ready to take control of **?**
your voiceover career

Then join me on this exciting, life-altering journey to discover the one and only brand that is you. As your brand coach, I'm going to hold you accountable. I'm going to ask you to shift your thinking and spend your time differently. I'm going to ask you some hard questions designed to nudge you out of your comfort zone. And I'm going to require that you be vulnerable and honest about who you really are — not who you'd like to be.

You're in the right place if:

- You are ready to maximize every aspect of your voiceover career
- You are a competitive voiceover talent
- You know your bottom line should be rising
- You could be working more
- You are not getting the opportunities you see your cohorts getting
- Buyers do not know you
- Agents are not interested in you
- Your current agent does not have you top of mind
- You understand that you are an entrepreneur
- You understand that talent alone is not enough

Entrepreneurs in all fields build their businesses on a rock solid foundation of smart business planning, a strategic marketing plan and a brand that can bang down doors. This book will start you on the path of developing that kind of brand and the kind of entrepreneurial thinking that will set you apart in the world of voiceover.

Are you ready? Then, as I like to tell my clients:

Chop, chop, Lollipop... Let's get this
V★PARTY Started !

Make yourself a voiceover branding journal. Maybe you're a spiral-notebook person. Or maybe you prefer a small cloth-covered bound book you can tuck in your bag. Maybe digital platforms, such as Evernote or Google docs, are your jam. Your branding journal will be a crucial tool for your creative process. So, whatever you do, select one that inspires you.

Once you have your branding journal, find a quiet place to spend a few minutes reflecting on what you've read so far. Write down your hopes and fears for the journey ahead.

Spend a few minutes each day in your journal reflecting on the ideas, brands, and people you are attracted to and how they are a clue to your personal brand. Carry your journal with you everywhere because you never know what might inspire you. Do all of the "Take Action" exercises in the following chapters in this one space. In the meantime, I've provided a mini-branding journal at the back of this book because I know you're a go-getter who'll want to get started right away!

Home   Demos   Videos   Clients   About   Contact

Traci Wilde VO

Sultry, smoky and sure to jump out and grab you.

Talent: Tracy Wilde

Tagline: "Sultry, smoky and sure to jump out and grab you."

What she's like: Kind of badass, rock and roll, and has an awesome hairdo — very stylized, with all these peacock colors. Blue hues. She commands the room. She's a little off-beat. Her tagline has a little bit of edge, just like she does.

Concept: Her name is Wilde, and Tracy actually is wild. A big, big personality. So it made sense to connect her brand with her name. The next question is: What's the best way to illustrate that? We didn't want to use leopard — that's cliché. But she likes to wear snakeskin and blue hues — peacock colors — like her hair.

Result: Tracy's brand matches her personality and her sound. It was an "aha" moment for people who already knew her, and when people meet her for the first time, it clicks.

What she says: "The most noticeable change since launching my brand is that both my confidence and my traffic to all profiles and websites have increased. People's reaction to my business card alone is instant! They recognize that the interaction they have with me is authentic and the brand that is on the card keeps that intrigue piqued. The process of developing my brand was so thorough, personal and layered it completely changed the dynamic of my business in every way. It brought out even more of my inner creativity and allowed me to really pinpoint my 'ground zero' business vision. I LOVE my brand!!! It makes me swoon."

CHAPTER 2:

PREPARE TO MEET YOUR INNER CELEBRITY

The secret to finding your swagger

Oprah, Richard Branson, Beyonce. Love 'em or hate 'em, you know who they are. A mere mention of these names conjures up an entire narrative in your mind. You know their story. You know their strengths and weaknesses. You know what they stand for. You know what they can do. How they move. What they sound like. You could probably sit down right now with a group of strangers and agree on five adjectives to describe these celebrities — their brands are burned into your brain.

That's no accident, of course. Their photos, outfits, words, and activities are chosen carefully to project an image — one that is carefully controlled by the PR machine that surrounds them. And while you may not have the resources of these celebrities, you do have what it takes to celebritize yourself.

This doesn't mean losing your authentic self. Quite the opposite. Oprah is Oprah — her brand didn't come out of nowhere. The well-defined brand she has built grew out of her essence. Remember Michelangelo's famous quote about the statue of David? The artist said the masterpiece was there in the block of marble the entire time. Similarly, your brand is in you already just waiting to see the light of day.

Too often I see people devoting their energy to developing a talent that isn't going to get heard. Think about that proverbial tree falling in the forest. Does anyone hear it? You don't want to be that tree. I don't want you to be that tree, either. The good news is: You don't have to be.

As your brand coach, I'm going to guide you through a process that will help you zero in on your true essence and chip away at anything that's getting in the way so you can become the voiceover achiever you were meant to be. That's what Oprah's team does for her. It's what I do for my voiceover clients, and it's what I'm going to do for you.

Voiceover is a global business, and that means there's a whole world of voiceover opportunities out there for you. Thanks to social media, you can reach any individual in the world. You can tweet to anybody. If you have something cool to look at, to listen to, to say — boom! — you can do it. No more waiting around for someone else to make it happen for you. And with home studios and portable rigs, you can take your talent anywhere.

All you need to do is figure out to how to break through and stand out from the crowd. How do you do that? The answer is simple: You need a brand.

The big questions in our industry used to be: Do you have a beautiful voice? Do you know how to act? Those are still important. But they're no longer enough. These days the question is: Are you brandable?

It's OK if you don't have a good answer to that question … yet. I'll give you another chance later.

● ● ●

Home   Demos   About   Clients   Contact

Steve Lawson.
Mankind VO.

When the nice guy is the coolest dude in the room.

Talent: Steve Lawson

Tagline: "Mankind VO. When the nice guy is the coolest guy in the room."

What he's like: Steve is truly undeniably nice and that is why his clients come back again and again. But he had been told that nice guys finished last and he should project a tougher image.

Concept: Nice guys finish first when they own their authenticity.

Result: Owning the fact that people hired him because he sounds nice and is nice brought Steve even more work.

My first job out of college, where I double-majored in film and psychology, was working as a receptionist at a talent agency in Minneapolis. On day one I watched a voiceover agent and I knew that was what I wanted to do. I took to voiceover like a duck to water. Soon I was promoted to agent at Wehmann and hatching a plan to move to Los Angeles, the voiceover capital of the world.

In LA, I was an agent at CESD (CED at the time), where I had the pleasure of working with the best in the biz. It felt like home. I loved the fast pace of voiceover. I loved the people — all so interesting, smart and entrepreneurial. And I loved creating success for them.

I had always been fascinated by the factors that create notoriety: What makes people stand out? How do creative people make their mark on the world? What spurs creativity in the first place? Now I had a front row seat.

In my 15 years as an agent, I saw the voiceover business go from recording on cassette tape to CD to the digital files of today. Back then, one of the biggest technological game changers was the fax machine. It seems quaint now, but the fax was our first glimpse of the global market we're living in now. Suddenly, instead of having copy messengered to us from local ad agencies, we could import copy from anywhere in the world. Suddenly, talent needed to stand out to compete not only in their own backyard but also nationwide.

My clients had a leg up because I had been preoccupied with helping talent stand out my entire career. My fascination with why some voiceover talent was successful, while their equally talented peers weren't, had led me to notice the 7 common denominators to voiceover success: those Seven Voiceover Superpowers I mentioned in the first chapter. As an agent, I went out of my way to make sure my clients had them all. And it paid off.

Debi Mae West was one of those early clients. The second I met her I could see her talent and her brand. She was a young woman working as a server and she had star potential. As soon as she got her brand right, her career took off and the momentum continues to build 20 years later.

"I could probably write an entire chapter about my brand's deep effect on my career," she says. "My career has flourished for 20 years. Ever since I first branded myself, I'm inspired year after year to have fun in the business to keep myself current with a great website, awesome demos and great marketing tools, to keep myself in the loop with clients, and staying genuine to my brand."

For Debi, that meant pushing the edge with all of our branding messages. For another talent, the right approach would be completely different. By matching Debi's brand to her personality, her voice and her sound, we hit on a winning formula that positioned her for long-term success.

1 **They had raw talent.** They were storytellers with great timing and a knack for improv.

2 **They sought out training.** They were curious lifelong learners who sought out the best teachers and they kept growing and deepening their skills year after year.

3 **They were committed.** They weren't dabbling in voiceover. Voiceover was their calling. I would frequently hear them say how lucky they are that they're in the best business in the world (I couldn't agree more!)

4 **They had business skills.** They realized voiceover isn't all about acting and they didn't shy away from the other aspects of this business. They saw themselves as entrepreneurs.

5 **The ability to make connections with others.** They understood and valued the power of relationships.

6 **They delegated and had a support team.** They saw what needs to be done in their career and delegated as needed. This allowed them to move their careers forward while spending as much of their precious time as possible in their zone of genius behind the microphone.

Eventually, I left L.A. to live the NORCal dream in San Francisco. I was working as an agent for JE Talent when I had my first daughter. It was the year 2000 during the commercial strike so it was a good time to take time off work for maternity leave. When I returned to work my boss was kind enough to let me bring my dear little Annabelle with me. There was an old recording booth complete with a glass window in my office. We turned it into a baby nursery where she could nap while I worked.

It was adorable. It also wasn't workable.

I really loved being a talent agent — the buzzing energy, phones ringing constantly, the intensity and energy of agents making deals, the push to get actors to bookings, the talent auditioning and picking up scripts. But with my attention divided between two incredibly demanding jobs, I quickly realized I couldn't be both the agent and the mom I wanted to be. I resigned.

Then the craziest thing happened. My actors kept contacting me, asking me to perform some of the "extra mile" tasks that I had for them as their agent. They didn't need me to be their agent per se, but they still needed the unique gift I had to offer. They needed help developing and marketing their brands. It was a lightbulb moment.

I vowed to spend the rest of my career doing everything in my power to propel voiceover actors to their most successful sweet spot using the power of branding. I created Celia Siegel Management - Branding, Marketing + Management for Voice Actors, and I've been doing that ever since.

I've been in this business for almost 30 years now. These days when I visit my agent friends I am still surprised by how quiet their offices are. The constant ringing of phones has been replaced by the quiet click-click-click of keyboards. Jobs are arranged via email. Demos posted online. But some things haven't changed. Every day is still a new adventure. Every shake-up creates opportunities. And I remain as passionate as ever about helping talent stand out from the crowd by teasing out the one-of-a-kind celebrity inside of each of them to create the personal brand that's perfect for them.

Which brings us back to that million dollar question:

Are you BRANDABLE?

I'll give you the answer:

YES.

Not only are you brandable, but your brand is already within you. It's in your DNA. You can't change your brand any more than Oprah could successfully reinvent herself as a computer geek. You can't be Oprah, or Beyonce or Richard Branson — those brands are already taken — but you can be something even better: the successful voiceover talent you and only you were meant to be.

If you follow the advice in this book and use the tools and techniques I've created to zero in on your personal brand, you will be able to chip away at all the obstacles that are preventing you from being a true voiceover achiever. The truth is: Your story is just as captivating as Oprah's or Richard Branson's or anyone else's. You deserve to find your inner celebrity and shine a spotlight on it for all the world to see.

● ● ●

Apple? Disney? Beyonce? Coke? Google? Toyota? Are you attracted to any of these brands? What does that say about you?

One of my favorite ways to help voice talent get in tune with the idea of being a brand is to encourage you to notice all the brands out in the world, track the ones you're drawn to and use those as clues to your own brand. As you go about your days, ask yourself, "What brands am I attracted to?" Write them down in your handy dandy Branding Journal. Then ask yourself, "What do I like about them?" Write that down, too.

Chances are the brand attributes you're most attracted to are attributes you bring to the table in your voiceover business on your very best day. As you create your brand, you can look to big, expensive brands you like for ideas of what would work for you.

"The reality is, the greatest companies in the world don't sell. They brand," says marketing guru Gary Vaynerchuk. "Think of Apple as a prime example... When, if ever, have you received an advertisement from Apple telling you to BUY their product? It never happens. Apple focuses on building a relationship that will last by deploying all of their energy into branding and showcasing how your life will change once you switch to iPhone. Their ads are about sharing an experience, about the simplicity and ease of use of their products. About how great it is to use the Mac. It's all about branding."

Speaking of Apple, that's one of the brands I find myself attracted to. I love their visuals. I love their message. Apple is about the future and innovation — being first to arrive. It feels comfortable to me. I feel like Apple people are my tribe. I'm also attracted to Zappos even though I don't love its aesthetic and I actually do most of my shoe shopping in physical stores. So what's the attraction? I adore how they take care of their customers. Noticing how Apple and Zappos branded themselves helped me make decisions about my own branding.

Once you've wrapped your mind around this new level of brand awareness, choose 10 brands that you're attracted to. These are the seeds of and clues to the brand we will build together in this book.

NOT LIKE THE OTHER.
GOOD BRANDING IS IN THE DETAILS.
SEE HOW THESE 3 WOMEN
DIFFERENTIATE THEMSELVES.

CHAPTER 3:

WHAT'S YOUR SUPERPOWER?

My superpower is helping you uncover yours

Branding is my life. I even dream brands. After a particular election, I dreamed that I rebranded the losing party — the one I had voted for — to empower it to succeed. I woke up laughing — of course, I was subconsciously using branding to cope with the defeat!

When people find out what I do, they all want to know what my personal brand is. I'll get to that in a bit, but first I'd like to take you back to the beginning — all the way back to my baby book.

My mom kept a meticulous baby journal that included the usual milestones: first smile, first tooth, first steps. But it was the other entries that gave clues to the person I would become and the personal brand I eventually would share with the world.

In one entry, she wrote that I had a peculiar habit of drifting away from the TV when shows came on but always stayed glued to the set for the commercials. In another, she talked about how I would focus on what was wonderful about pretty much everything under the sun and then talk it up to anyone who would listen.

As I grew older, my favorite sport became guessing people's stories.

I've played this game with camp counselors, bus drivers, servers, college professors, accountants and real estate agents — you name it — and I have an uncanny knack for getting the stories right. But that's not the best part. The best part is that each story — each person — is just as fascinating as the next. Each of us has a story to tell. My passion is to help bring these stories to the forefront in a truly authentic and compelling way.

Of course, I didn't start out knowing what my path would be. My talents and interests drew me to the world of voiceover. As I've mentioned, early in my career as a talent agent, I became fascinated by the factors that led to success. Everyone I worked with had talent but some were far more successful than others. While the reasons for this gap eluded them, I recognized what was happening and saw the solution. Both the big solution: branding. And the specific brand solution for each client.

This is when I realized I had a knack for seeing brands — for tapping into the essence of individuals so they could shine their brightest. This was my superpower. Superman had x-ray vision; I had brand vision. When I started my business I decided it was time to own this unique gift. Armed with years of voiceover industry insider experience, I set out to change the world one person, one talent, one brand at a time.

I formed Celia Siegel Management to provide a clear path to entrepreneurial success for talent I knew had the potential to reach higher heights. I've been doing that ever since. I've spent much of my career developing proven, fruitful branding strategies that empower and propel the voiceover careers of my clients. This comes as naturally to me as taking those first baby steps. And it makes me happy.

And now I'm extending my passion for helping those in the voiceover industry find their branding power source by writing this book. You, too, have a personal brand that was already in you when you were taking your first steps. And when you take the time to examine those characteristics that are uniquely you, you, too, can build a brand, a business and a life that makes you happy. It is my firm belief that once you get your brand story right, everything in your life falls into place.

My definition of brand is the story you want to tell the world about who you really are and what the real you can give. Not a super perfect story about who you would be if only you were flawless. To successfully brand yourself, you need to be willing to show not the perfect version of yourself — not who you wish you could be — but who you really are.

So who am I really? What is my brand? The answer is: brand intuitive. I view the world through a brand prism and see what's wonderful inside people. I use this talent to help them see it, too, so they can broadcast it to the world.

Once I strike upon a person's essence, I see the complete brand finished — it comes together like a picture in my head — and I know how to communicate that to a designer so it comes to life as I envision it. When I show the client, nine times out of 10 they literally jump up and down. This is the joy that comes from being seen for who you truly are.

When I work with clients, I create a main brand — an umbrella brand — then tweak how it's presented for each particular audience. When approaching creative types, you can be more playful and flippant. With corporations, more straightforward and businesslike. It's the same brand, packaged in a slightly different way.

"Successful brands are not static. Nor are they rooted in static things, like logos, stationery, and slogans," says Joan Baker, co-founder of Society of Voice Arts and Sciences with her husband Rudy Gaskins. "Brands are dynamic entities that are fueled by creating value for others. As a voice actor, your primary value lies in your voice acting ability, an effective means for delivering your service, and your relationship skills.

"Branding begins with cultivating genuine value for the audience you seek to serve, i.e., agents, casting directors and buyers. Branding continues by nurturing and expanding your value to accommodate your audience's evolving needs. Your audience is constantly evolving and brands have to evolve with them or be a step ahead, ready to serve when the audience arrives. Elasticity and innovation allow brands to do this."

But that doesn't mean you try to please everyone. Here's the truly tricky thing about branding: If you do it right some people aren't going to like it.

In order for branding to work, you have to tell the truth. My job is to give clients a brand that makes them say, "Aha! That's my message!" But sometimes they are reluctant to show their true selves even to me.

I had a client I adored (and still do!), but creating her brand was a struggle. Christian Taylor insisted that her brand present an idealized version of herself and I couldn't talk her out of it. She wouldn't reveal her whole true self because she was focused on looking perfect. We created her brand. It was safe and pretty. But I didn't feel it. There were no sharp edges, no dark side, nothing to separate her from the pack. She's a good actress, so she jumped up and down convincingly when I showed it to her.

I saw her a few months later at a conference. She came up to me after my presentation and said, "Celia, I just listened to your presentation and I saw all your beautiful brands. I don't like my brand." I was like, "What?!" because I'm used to the jumping up and down — not this. I said, "Dang it. Let's fix it."

We started over. We went through the Voiceover Brand Finder process I developed. It's a series of questions I use with my clients to help zero in on their brand and create their brand story (I'll walk you through the same process in Chapter 5). We did it and came up with a few ideas. All were authentic, but one stood out — it was completely her: the ultimate neighbor lady, the reliable, resourceful person next door you could always go to, whether to soothe a worry or borrow a cup of sugar.

Again, she resisted. "I can't do that," she told me, "That's too middle-aged." I wasn't going to let her make the same mistake again. I told her, "This neighbor lady is beautiful. I want her on my block. I yearn for that woman on my block who I can trust, who I can trust with my story, who I can borrow sugar from, who knows how to make a pie, who would watch my kid if I had an emergency. That person is gorgeous. That's how you sound and that's who you are."

The next time I saw her was at another conference. This time she wasn't in the audience — she had a booth that people were flocking to. She was all apple pies and stain remover and handing out wooden spoons. She was the ultimate neighbor lady and everyone loved her.

When she saw me, she said, "Celia, my business is so great. People are coming to me and hiring me. I am middle-aged. I'm amazing and I'm wise and I'm still cute as a button. I had to let go and be authentic to get where I am now.

Christian Taylor
Neighbor Lady VO
Nobody tells a story, soothes a worry, or supplies the sugar quite like Christian.

That's the biggest challenge of branding — dropping the need to be perfect. Being perfect is exhausting and not as interesting or appealing as being real. It's like trying to squeeze into a pair of beautiful shoes that are two sizes too small. Now Christian says, "My new branding fits like my favorite flip-flops and makes me feel fabulous. It gives me pride, strength, and presence in the noisy VO marketplace and that makes me exceedingly happy."

A few years ago, Katie DeGabriel came to me saying she was feeling like a voiceover imposter because she was new to the business. To combat this fraud syndrome, she hired me to develop her brand. We went through the usual process and she was forthcoming ... to a point.

Her life was a little messy, she told me, but deep down at her core she was a Zen yoga master and she wanted a brand that reflected that. That quality was definitely in her — an important part of her personality — and we launched a serene, tranquil, ohm-like brand. "That is so me!" she said. "Thank you!"

But in reality, it was only part of her story. A year later, she came clean and admitted she wasn't actually a Zen yoga master but an overscheduled single mom who longed for a more Zen-like existence. "I'm late for everything. I have stains on my clothes," she confessed. "I want to be serene but my life is anything but." Aha, this was her real authentic self. We rebranded her with the tagline "Maternally cool. Eternally real." The visuals depict a many-armed mom a la the goddess Kali trying to do it all. Guess who's bookings went through the roof?

Katie recently sent me a thank-you email for helping her peel back the layers of the onion to reveal "the true me, my authentic brand: the single mom doing voiceover work."

"I love my brand because it's me, my truth, and I'm finally OK showing that to the VO industry," she wrote.

● ● ●

Katie DeGabriel VO
Maternally cool. Eternally real.

We think that being perfect makes us attractive, desirable, hirable. But the truth is that only by showing our true imperfect selves do we attract our tribe. There is magic on the dark side.

What are you really terrible at? Like super painfully awful at? There is a pot of gold 180 degrees away from that. Your brilliance can always be found on the flipside of your weaknesses.

I'll go first.

If you spin me around, I will be lost. I can't navigate my way anywhere I haven't been at least a hundred times already. I can't even find my table at a restaurant when I come out of the bathroom. Don't even get me started on airports. I tried for years to become a directionally savvy person. It was a constant struggle.

One day while I was busy driving around trying to find the new coffee shop without directions, it hit me: I was watering a dead plant. This was sucking energy away from what comes naturally to me — being creative. You might spend years running from your shadow side. But you can't escape it. So you might as well stop running and embrace it.

GPS changed my life. And I'm probably the only person ever who asks, "May I have a table near the bathroom?" and "Would you mind if I follow you out of the airport?" These adaptations let me spend more time and brainpower doing what I am meant to be doing: tuning in and finding the authentic brand in each person I meet.

There's a reason you picked up this book. It is no accident. Like me, you have a message, a beautiful message to share with the world. You also have a mission — the world needs your gifts. And you yearn to attract your tribe. We all do. It's human nature.

But a lot of us work alone now. We're on our screens, doing the hard work of being a voiceover entrepreneur. It's not nine to five; it's 24/7. Technology can be a trap, a cage that isolates us and distracts us from who we really are. So what's the answer? How do we share our message when we're flying solo all the time?

By remembering that this miracle called the Internet is actually a superhighway. That very same thing that puts us in isolation, clips our wings and leaves us less than fulfilled can actually help us attract our tribe. On this superhighway, you can go anywhere, meet anyone. You may find your tribe on the other side of the country. Doesn't that sound fun?

I'd like you to take a minute, shut your eyes and think about what your mission is. What were you put on this earth to do? Who do you want to serve? Spend a few minutes meditating on how your whole life story has brought you to this mission. Feel the joy and the humanity of fulfilling that mission. Sit with that feeling. Savor it.

Now that you have that feeling, I want to ask a tough question: Do you want to walk away from that and settle for Plan B? Or do you want to put everything you've got into making Plan A — your mission on this great big planet full of all sorts of people — happen?

Your inner skeptic may be insisting on a practical Plan B. I urge you to shove that naysayer aside for a few moments and visualize your heart's desire. It feels great, doesn't it?

Are you prepared to show — not the perfect, aspirational, Photoshopped version of yourself but your true vulnerable self? Are you ready to be honest — not about what you wish you could do for a living but what you really want to do? Are you prepared to connect — not with some idealized customer but with your tribe?

I challenge you to really step outside into the light and show the real you. That's what your tribe wants. As for me, I want the whole world to be branded. I will sleep better at night knowing more people are finding success and happiness by getting their brand right. When you get your brand right, you'll sleep better, too.

● ● ●

One of the services I provide to clients is being a sounding board, someone to talk to as they go through the challenging process of self-exploration required to uncover their brand. And even though you're tackling this whole branding thing DIY, it's crucial that you, too, have a sounding board — someone who will commit to meeting with you regularly to discuss your branding journey. Ideally, this person would be a fellow VO talent embarking on his or her own branding journey so you could return the favor. No matter what, it has to be a smart, business-minded person you feel comfortable with. One caveat: Avoid loved ones who are too invested in your success and happiness to provide the kind of support you will need.

Start by writing down a list of potential brand buddies in your branding journal. Circle your top three contenders and then reach out to see if they're available and interested in committing for three months. Once you have your brand buddy, invite them to tea, coffee or kombucha in a celebratory kickoff. It's going to be fun!

CHAPTER 4:

WHY YOU NEED A BRAND

It's good for your business (and even your soul)

To be successful in the voiceover industry you need to shift your focus from resume-building to brand-building. This can feel soul-crushing, I realize. You're already working around the clock. You don't need another thing to do. That inner skeptic is there resisting: "I don't want to be a brand. I don't want to advertise. I don't want a business plan. I just want to do good work."

I get it. But I'm not going to let you off the hook.

Take a moment to look at the people who are succeeding in our world today. Look at our current president, the YouTubers, the video game stars, the business leaders. You don't have to like them to see that they are all passionate and authentic and imperfect. This makes them interesting, and people buy interesting.

Celebrity branding expert Jeetendr Sehdev sheds light on this phenomenon in his book The Kim Kardashian Principle: Why Shameless Sells. "If Hollywood has taught me one thing, it's the danger of following the pack and disappearing into a sea of sameness," Sehdev writes. "Hollywood has always been a town of transformation, where people come to forget who they are and become who they want to be. But Kim Kardashian has turned that on its head. Today, it is more important to be the person you've always been, flaws and all, and no one knows this better than Kim."

The same is true in voiceover. I'm not advocating being 100 percent shameless, of course, and I'm definitely not advocating keeping up with the Kardashians. What I am advocating is being loud and proud about who you really are. We live in a world where authentic brands capture the prize.

So what is a brand anyway? I like to start with marketer and author Seth Godin's definitions. Godin says a brand is "the set of expectations, memories, stories, and relationships that, taken together, account for a consumer's decision to choose one product or service over another." His definition of a personal brand is slightly different: "a story, a set of emotions and expectations and a stand-in for how we think and feel about what you do."

When it comes to voiceover, there are lots of ways to think about it:

- Your brand is how you intrigue people and make them want to know you.
- Your brand is how others perceive you.
- Your brand is your network, your status updates, your content and your social sharing.
- Your brand is your story.
- Your brand is how you tip off others on what it's like to work with you.
- Your brand is your reputation.
- Your brand is the first impression you make.
- Your brand is knowing who you are.
- Your brand is knowing who you're not.
- You are a brand.

In short, your brand is what separates you from everybody else out there competing in this industry. To succeed in voiceover it is an absolute necessity to tell a story about yourself that helps you stand out from the rest of the crowd.

Great brands are like snowflakes, thumbprints, and individual personalities. Branding allows you to take personal control of your story. Successful brands are not pulled out of thin air — they sprout out of the seeds of the authentic self and must be carefully tended to reach their full potential. That's what successful celebrities do. And you can do it, too.

Just as it's important to know who you're not when zeroing in on your personal brand, it's also crucial to understand what a brand is not: A brand is not a logo or a design or a wrapper. Those are mere markers of a brand's existence. These brand shadows — and how they're designed — are important once you have your brand in place. But just as it takes more than a ten-gallon hat to be a cowboy, it takes more than a cool font to make a brand. Design is essential but design alone is not brand. It is one of the tools you use later to implement your brand, and we'll get to that in a future chapter.

Have you heard of Maslow's Hierarchy of Needs? In 1943 psychologist Abraham Maslow published a paper called "A Theory of Human Motivation" in the journal Psychological Review. It was about how people are motivated to achieve certain needs. His idea was that in order to achieve self-actualization — the most exalted state of being — humans needed more basic needs met first. His hierarchy is often presented as a pyramid.

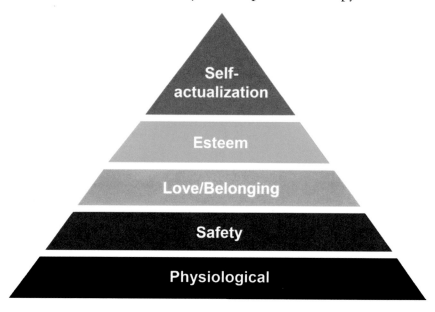

An authentic personal brand is a pathway to voiceover self-actualization. It can help propel you to the top of that pyramid by first helping you gain confidence, self-esteem, and respect. But first, you'll need to develop a brand mindset, to start seeing the world through a brand prism. You don't need to geek out to the extent that I do, but you do need a personal brand.

When you start thinking of yourself as a brand, you'll start doing better. And once you've done the hard work of personal branding, your brand will start working for you even when you're not working. Your brand will take on a life of its own, telling the story of your unique gifts even as you sleep.

Someone recently asked me a good question: Can a great brand propel a mediocre talent to success? Yes, and it happens all the time. But a great brand cannot sustain mediocrity. Or as Vaynerchuk puts it: "You can market your ass off, but if your product sucks, you're dead."

Conversely, can awesome voiceover talent reach their full potential without a great brand? No, you will never reach your full potential without a great brand. The magic happens when competitive talent is paired with competitive branding.

I hate to see a talented person in a super weak brand.

Recently a new potential client sent me a link to his website. His website was terrible. I made negative assumptions about his talent because of the poor branding. Then I pressed play. What a shocker! His voice was like butter. His timing was great. He was amazing, but his website was sending a message that he wasn't worthwhile. And it made me so freaking sad because most people never move past first impressions. Most people wouldn't have pressed play.

How many talented voiceover actors are hiding their amazingness behind crummy marketing materials? How many of you are busting your butts to make up for all the positive connections you're losing because of an ugly website? How many of you are considering driving for Uber to make ends meet because you're not getting enough work even though you know you have what it takes? Ugh!

This is why you need a brand: Because whether or not you have intentionally created a brand, you have one. Make your life easier. Make sure your branding authentically reflects your talent and who you are. The decision makers in our wonderful industry are busy. A good brand will let them see instantly that they're in good hands with your talent.

● ● ●

HOW TO DO A NICHE BRAND

**What if you're not a jack- or jill-of-all-trades?
Check out how these two talent branded
themselves specifically for audiobooks/narration.**

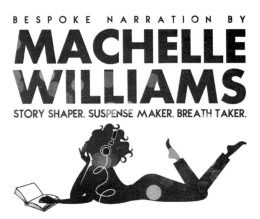

B E S P O K E   N A R R A T I O N   B Y

MACHELLE WILLIAMS

STORY SHAPER. SUSPENSE MAKER. BREATH TAKER.

"The work we did on my brand has absolutely helped me perfect my
'elevator speech.'" When prospective clients ask me what I do or
what I deliver, I immediately know what to say to paint a picture of my
narration vs. my competition. It was a great exercise. I am so glad I did
it.

"Creating this brand with Celia is one of the most important and best decisions I've ever made for my career. The brand was built from insights we uncovered in the process of creating my business plan. That step made a big difference. One thing we discovered early on was that the types of work I most enjoyed, and had the most success in, all referred to the actor as a narrator, not voiceover. Specifically, audiobook narration and e-learning narration. We decided to use 'Andi Arndt, Narrator' as my title to signal to potential clients that I was focused on their niche of the market. It felt right.

My old site felt like it could have been anybody's. My new site felt like a natural extension of me and my work, something I was proud and excited to share with people. Celia helped me turn a trait that had been a negative with some clients (calm energy) into a positive, branded statement about what I bring to a narration project."

TAKE ACTION:

FRIENDS WITH BRAND BENEFITS

Identify 10 or so people you trust from different parts of your life. Include some from the voiceover industry and some from other parts of your life — your agent, a client, friends, family, a colleague, a neighbor and especially anyone who is good with words. Ask them to spend five minutes to compose a short email describing you — what they love about you as well as your challenges. The first things that come to mind — no sugar-coating.

One of the cool parts of being in the voiceover industry is that you know a bunch of crazy-creative people. This means that the people who know you best are a wonderful resource as you seek brand clarity. Be sure to tap them for this exercise — especially your writer friends as they are especially good at this.

Then, while you're waiting for their responses, try to guess what they're going to say. How are they going to describe you? Take out your brand journal and write it down.

After you have the responses, write down all the adjectives in your branding journal. Were your predictions right? Do any words surprise you? Do any pop out at you? Notice any patterns? Where is the overlap between you as a human being and how you use your voice talent?

Star the ones that make you nod in agreement — even if you're a little embarrassed about them, even if they make you squirm. Remember, this is not about being perfect. This is about being you.

CHAPTER 5:

UNCOVER YOUR BRAND

Steps to finding the story of awesomeness that is you

Now for the fun part! Really. You've already been dipping your toes into uncovering your brand. It's time to plunge yourself into the deep end as I walk you through several exercises I use with my clients.

It's crucial that you build your voiceover business in the right order. The keystone is — you guessed it — your brand. The exercises in this chapter will help you build your brand step by step. And it's going to take some real time and commitment. When I work with clients we spend many hours going through the brand discovery phase — a process that's designed to compel you to get real with yourself, to truly focus on who you are and get in touch with your authentic self.

Have you ever gone to someone's website and it looks professional — attractive design, good functionality — but it doesn't give you any sense of the person? We see it all the time. Voice talent who throw up a website before they do the branding work. It's like creating a voice demo right after you take your first community college "Intro to Voiceover" class. Too soon!

You'll have much better results when you build your website and all other marketing and business materials on a solid foundation. A strong brand helps you be intentional about how you are perceived — it becomes your business style guide.

"Working in the VO community is amazing," says Gerald Griffith, president and founder of Voiceovercity. "There are so many different experiences and backgrounds. Whichever stage they happen to be in, I inevitably find myself talking with them about how they see their business and how they want their clients to see them.

Griffith says there are a few things all talent have in common, whether they're seasoned professionals or just getting started:

- They struggle to understand the difference in things they control — like their website, voiceover demo or logo design vs. the things they don't control like whether there's a market for their voice or whether agents have a need for their particular sound on their roster.
- They have trouble grasping that their brand is more than just their business cards or website. It's everything about them and how people perceive them across all channels — from how they handle phone calls to the type of email address they use. Everything communicates the type of service provider they are.
- They underestimate the value of relationships within the industry. Talent, agents, directors or producers all have the ability to advocate for success or sound an alarm of caution. "It behooves everyone to give thought to what and how they treat others," Griffith says.

Are you excited? If not, you're not alone. Being the branding geek that I am, I am always surprised that most people don't share my enthusiasm for doing branding exercises. But I am going to ask you set aside your skepticism. If you unfurrow that brow and embrace the idea that branding can be fun, you just might enjoy yourself. I'm also going to remind you again that your brand is already 100 percent within you. You don't have to change who you are. You don't have to be a master of design. You don't have to be a spin doctor. All you have to do is be honest. That's not easy, but it is freeing.

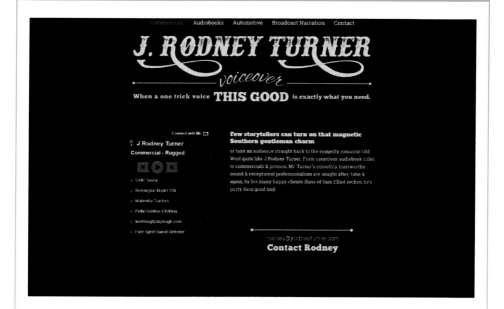

Talent: J. Rodney Turner

Tagline: "When a one-trick voice this good is exactly what you need."

What he's like: J. Rodney has a gorgeous gravelly Southern accent.

Concept: When I met J. Rodney, we talked a lot about whether his accent was a limitation. And then we determined it was his greatest asset. Rather than watering down who he was, we decided to own it.

Result: J. Rodney's so-called limitation became his greatest asset.

What he says: "The process of creating my brand was an awesome experience. It allowed me to see myself more clearly. The most important element that came out of this process was knowing, for myself, what type of scripts and jobs I would have a very high percentage chance of being able to book — and those I needed to simply leave for someone else. That, in and of itself, allowed me to be more free in the auditioning process as well as the other areas of working to build a VO career."

"The key to success in this business, let alone any business, is the 'point of view,'" says Wesley Stevens, CEO, and Founder of VOX, Inc. "It is the individual's unshakeable foundation of personal authenticity. Getting to this place requires the deep dive into self, the fearless honesty to look at who and what we are, what we're good at, what we're not, where we resonate, how we impact. It really is a soul search. In this business, that cuts through more than anything else. The voice is a mirror of the soul, there is no smoke and mirror game that can replace authenticity.

"The reason a celebrity is a success and the top 20 percent of voice actors make over 80 percent of the revenue is that they walk in the room a brand (even if that is just inside their head) and they deliver a bill of goods that the buyer knows and trusts — consistently. They can come to any script, any character, any project and lay their 'take' on it. And they do it without the wobbly and worrisome self-doubt of, 'Was that right?' 'Did I get it?' 'Did you like that?' They end their sentences, their delivery, their work with a period. Done.

How do we get to these places of strength and knowing? We get quiet. We listen, we watch, we study. In these places we observe and we start to shape and refine the sense of self. In business, this self is the brand. I have watched it over and over in the studio, the moment just before the perfect delivery — silence. And the moment after, the pause after the period — silence. In between these rests the music of the authentic voice, a lifetime in the making; shaped by the ability to listen to your place in the big picture."

This is what I want for my clients and for you, VoiceOverAchiever. I want you to do the hard work of finding your brand because it will boost every area of your life — your confidence, your relationships, your bank account, the quality of your work, your passion for all you do. Sound good? Thought so. Let's go!

PERSONAL BRANDING D.I.Y.

EXERCISE 1: BRAND FINDER
12 questions specifically designed to help you begin to uncover the brand inside you.

Branding allows you to tell your story in a way that is entertaining, concise and specific. The trick is to focus in on exactly what that story is and then to emphasize important aspects of that story that your ideal customer will find interesting. I developed this Brand Finder tool with that in mind. And I use it to kickstart the brand discovery process with all of my clients. Spending time grappling with — and answering — these questions is a crucial first step toward getting at the heart of your brand story.

GO!

When you're ready, take out your Brand Journal and write your answers to the following questions:

1 **What do you want to accomplish?** (You must know where you are headed in order to get there. Be as specific as possible.)

2 **What makes you competitive and differentiates you from other talent?** (Voiceover is an extremely competitive business. Knowing what makes you unique will allow you to carve out your voiceover niche. Sameness makes every single audition like the lottery. Uniqueness makes you stand out, which gives you an edge.)

3 **If you could only audition for one style of copy what would you want it to be?** (Your main brand needs to appeal to your core audience. Pick a genre and start there. Nuanced changes in approach can be made for other genres.)

4 What would you like advertising agencies/buyers to know about you and your style? (In other words, why should anyone hire you? A clear answer to this question is imperative. If you don't have one, you have work to do.)

5 How would you describe your current image? (What feels great? What's missing? What needs an upgrade? Be tough on yourself. Only by assessing yourself honestly will you be able to make improvements.)

6 In your opinion, is there anything about your image that feels outdated or off-base? (What message are you sending out now? Do you send the wrong message? What could be enhanced or improved upon?)

7 What words do you associate with your signature sound? (Use detailed language to describe your voice. Be honest. Be bold. You'll be doing a lot more of this type of thing.)

8 What colors, textures, moods or metaphors come to mind about your voice/image (your voice/image sounds, feels or is like _____?) (This is my sneaky way to get colorful images from you that you can use to create visuals.)

9 What popular cultural icons (famous people, movie stars/eras, popular commercial products/trends, etc.), contemporary or historical, could you align with your voice? (What does your story have in common with theirs? Find descriptions of the items on your list and note any clues to your own brand.)

10 What kind of music, fashions, stores, and what area of the country does your voice feel most comfortable in? (Look at how the entities on your list advertise and again scour the ads for clues to your brand.)

11 What brands (can be any product or service including other voice talent brands) do you personally like and why? (This one is huge! If you are attracted to someone or something, you see your ideal self aka brand in it. For instance, I love Apple because it is visionary, well designed and a hub for an entire community. That's what I am on a great day!!

I love Zappos. Not for the shoes — I could find shoes anywhere — but for the culture and the delightful customer service! I love giving that kind of service!

I love Birchbox because it's well designed, appealing and tailored just to me. See how you play this game? Spend some serious time noticing and creating around this concept. You can **find inspiration in the multi-million-dollar brands that you love.)**

12 **Make a list of all the character voices/roles, networks and commercial products that you see yourself as a perfect fit for.**

13 **Write a rough and brief voice talent and career bio.** Just a couple paragraphs. You will edit and infuse this bio with your brand later, so don't sweat the writing too much at this point. Include notable details about your voice and work/professional qualities (feel free to pull from your answers to questions above) as well as your home studio info, where you are located and any personal or professional tidbits that might interest a potential buyer.

REFLECT!

Study and analyze your answers. Look for words, phrases, and ideas that especially resonate with you. Highlight those and rewrite them in your Brand Journal.

Talent: Nazia Chaudhry

Tagline: "Easy going glamour ... effervescent charm."

What she's like: Her nickname is Naz. She's a jazz singer. She does on-camera in addition to VO. She never leaves the house without looking like she's had a session with a professional makeup artist and stylist. She's bubbly, versatile and easy to work with.

Concept: When someone has a lot going on it can be a challenge to boil it down to their essence, but it's always there. In her case, at the heart of everything she does is effortlessness and warmth.

Result: We paired this tagline with her photo and — bingo — you know exactly who she is. From that core, she was able to build a big website showing all her facets.

What she says: "I met Celia at the exact moment I was feeling overwhelmed with my career branding, since there are so many facets to my work aside from voice acting. My brand has been a complete game changer in all aspects of my career."

46

MIKE COOPER VOICEOVER
The guy next door. Only better. And British.

DEMOS   WORK   CLIENTS   REVIEWS   ABOUT   CONTACT

► Commercial

► Documentary Narration

WELCOME!

I'm Mike Cooper - a British voice over artist, now based in America. Allow me to explain (with the help of this whiteboard animation...)

Talent: Mike Cooper

Tagline: "Mike Cooper Voiceover. The guy next door. Only better. And British."

What he's like: Mike is smart, hip and in the know and happens to have a British accent.

Concept: This playful twist on the cliché of the guy next door sets Cooper, who lives in the U.S., apart from the pack of "regular guys" and sets him up to be a memorable go-to for buyers seeking his accent.

Result: This brand helped Mike corner the market as a smart, cool British guy. Anytime you can use humor and a twist on saying what we have all heard, it helps to get the message across.

PERSONAL BRANDING D.I.Y.

EXERCISE 2: TESTIMONIALS
What your customers say about you is pure gold, so let it shine.

Whether shopping for an appliance or a pair of shoes, savvy customers read online reviews. They're looking for "social proof," the marketing term for reassurance from others that they're making a good decision. Social proof gives us a sense of safety as we fork over our hard-earned money for a new product. The same is true in the voiceover industry.

Your customers will feel better about hiring you when they see social proof that you deliver. That's reason No. 1 for collecting compliments. Testimonials also often contain words, phrases, and impressions that can form the foundation of your brand. So how do you go about gathering these powerful customer stories? It's actually quite easy.

As you go about your busy days, I bet people often say nice things about your work. You probably don't even notice much of the time. You say thanks and move on. The trick to gathering testimonials is to make it a habit to catch people complimenting you, and then asking them if you can use it as a testimonial. Something like: "Hey, you are so sweet! Thank you so much! That really means a lot to me. Would you mind if I use that as a testimonial?" Or if you notice someone posting something nice about your work on social media, follow up: "Hey! I'm so happy that you were happy with my work! Do you mind if I share this little story on my website? That would really help me out."

The best testimonials are straightforward and not overly promotional, include real results, provide social proof for your product and help you tell your brand story to future clients. A good testimonial tells the story of what it was like for somebody to work with you in a way that builds trust for others to do the same. Sometimes this happens organically. Other times it takes some coaxing. You may need to prompt them with a follow-up question to turn a quick compliment into a story. The goal is to make it as easy on your contacts as possible while encouraging them to craft the sort of testimonial that will sell you.

Most people are happy to help, so there's no need to be shy about asking. Don't worry if you don't hear back right away. Chances are they meant to respond and just got caught up with other things. It's OK to follow up after a week or so. And even if you don't get a testimonial out of the exchange, paying attention to how your customers describe you can provide important clues to your brand and fodder for your brand story. And the very act of reaching out and saying thank you is good for your business.

I recommend using your Brand Journal to track nice feedback to remind yourself to follow-up. Soon gathering testimonials will become second nature and a seamless part of running your voiceover enterprise. In the meantime, you can take simple actions to jumpstart this new habit.

GO!

Make a list of everybody who you've ever worked with and send an email prompt out to each of them asking for a written testimonial. Some prompts you can use:

- How was it to work with me?
- How was the final project?
- What was the moment that you knew that the voiceover was going to work out with me?
- What happened with this project after I did my part?

REFLECT!

Study and analyze the testimonials. Look for words, phrases, and ideas that especially resonate with you. Highlight those and rewrite them in your Brand Journal.

PERSONAL BRANDING D.I.Y.

EXERCISE 3: QUICK 100
You are 100 different things.
What are they?

At the beginning of each year, I devote a big chunk of time to long-term planning. I use a planner that has a section that prompts me to list as quickly as I can 100 things I want to do that year just for fun. Because I love my work so much, doing an exercise that's strictly about having fun is challenging for me. A hundred is so many! But this practice has changed my life by nudging me out of my comfort zone and forcing me to be intentional about having fun. Now each year I enjoy looking back and seeing all the fun I've had.

Inspired by this annual 100, I started asking my clients to do a different kind of quick 100 that's even more painful. In fact, it's downright outrageous to the point of being silly. So why do I make this request? Because being willing to get way out of your comfort zone is what it takes to create a really good brand. And it works.

I challenge you to complete this exercise and to keep going even after your brain starts to hurt. Because just like with fun things to do, the really special one sometimes comes at the end.

GO!

Set a timer for 15 minutes and list 100 (yes, 100!) adjectives that describe what's different about you. We've included a bunch right here to get you started.

frank
generous
amiable **witty**
exuberant resourceful
sympathetic **rational** humble
calm **diligent** flamboyant eccentric
gregarious **considerate** charismatic
passionate
sincere compassionate reliable **sensible**
inventive impartial philosophical **eclectic**
calm adaptable persistent **ambitious**
improv **real** empathetic humble persistent
courageous resourceful courteous
compassionate exuberant **modest** passionate
conversational **eccentric** amiable
takes direction well gregarious chic
genuine affectionate **reliable**
smooth adventurous
practical gravelly
inventive **actor**

REFLECT!

Study and analyze your answers. Highlight at least 10 words that ring the truest and rewrite them in your Brand Journal.

Talent: Iesha Nyree

Tagline: "Sparkling. Wondrous. Loveable. Limitless."

What she's like: Her sound is loveable, her character reads are wondrous and she has contagiously fun energy in the booth.

Concept: This brand is simply an exclamation of Iesha's sparkling wonder.

Result: This brand has helped Iesha grow her contact list and her business. It gives her an extra bounce to her step because it is so playful and in her DNA.

What she says: "The most surprising change I've seen since launching my brand is how many times I'll get a request for an audition or a gig simply because someone noticed my branding and decided to check out more. I learned that a good brand goes beyond just a strong first impression — it is a sizzling elevator speech mixed with a charismatic smile that draws people in!"

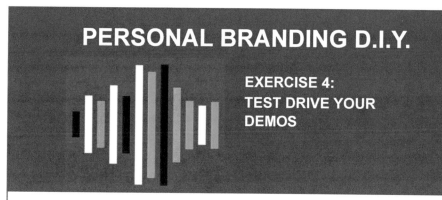

PERSONAL BRANDING D.I.Y.

**EXERCISE 4:
TEST DRIVE YOUR
DEMOS**

This is an adaptation of a small-group branding session I do with my clients. When I host these workshops, everyone brings their demos and we listen to them as a group. We write down the words that flash in our minds as we listen. At the end, we share, paying special attention to themes.

It's important to get outside of yourself and listen to yourself as a product. Your Brand Buddy can be a great help in figuring out the feelings that your voice conjures up for listeners. And if you can gather a larger group together, all the better. This is a great exercise to try if you meet with other actors regularly or have a workout group, book club, etc., that's willing to indulge you.

GO!

Make a special two-hour date with your Brand Buddy for a listening session and discussion. Before the meeting listen to your demos and take notes on why you would hire you (or not!). Listen again at the meeting with your Brand Buddy and discuss why you would hire you. Does your buddy agree? Why or why not? Discuss. Take notes in your Brand Journal as you do this.

REFLECT!

Study and analyze your notes. Look for words, phrases, and ideas that especially resonate with you. Highlight those and rewrite them in your Brand Journal.

Home   Demos   Videos   About   Clients   Contact   Blog

Dustin Ebaugh

HONEST TO GOODNESS VO
Bringing your brand to life with a soulful connection.

Talent: Dustin Ebaugh

Tagline: "Honest to Goodness VO. Bringing your brand to life with a soulful connection."

What he's like: Dustin is a real charmer. And he's super talented. And he grew up in the middle of nowhere.

Concept: With a little wink to his upbringing, we convey the honest earnestness of Dustin's voice.

Result: With this approachable brand and the talent to back it up, Dustin's client relationships have flourished.

What he says: "I suppose the most surprising change I've seen since taking on my brand and owning it, is that it's changed not only how I market, but to whom. I'm much more focused now. I know who I am, how I'm represented in the marketplace with my brand and now marketing is easier and less stressful because all I have to remember is to be true to myself and my brand."

EXERCISE 5:
20 REASONS TO HIRE YOU
When you get hired it's for a reason,
but do you know what that reason is?

We're back to our old friend the common denominator. Anybody who hires you is going to be a creative and expressive person. In addition to including your own perception, be sure to include comments from your agent or the buyer and pay special attention to commonalities.

GO!

Write down your last 20 jobs, leaving space between each one. Why did you get hired for each one? Write it down.

REFLECT!

Study and analyze your list. Look for commonalities. Highlight those and rewrite them in your Brand Journal.

PERSONAL BRANDING D.I.Y.

EXERCISE 6: PIN IT TO WIN IT
Let's get visual, visual!

Pinterest is an amazing tool for creating a vision of your brand. And it's fun to go crazy and pin images of everything you are attracted to — anything that gives you that "a-ha" feeling and feels like you. Do this with images, with fonts, with colors. Spend some time with the companies that you were attracted to in the previous exercise and pin whatever speaks to you. Don't stop to assess your pins. Just keep pinning! Then, once you've exhausted yourself doing this, take a rest. Then go back and do the final step with fresh eyes. It should make you feel happy and inspired to collect all these things you would be proud to associate with. This is the beginning of your style guide.

GO!

Create a My Brand Pinterest board. Then get ready to have fun pinning like a madman for at least an hour in the following three categories. Don't overthink. Include websites, social media, graphics, print ads. Everything that inspires you. Pin it all!

- Pin all the images that you are attracted to.
- Then do the same with fonts.
- Then do the same focusing on colors.

REFLECT!

Study and analyze your pins. Look for images, colors, words, phrases, and ideas that especially resonate with you. Look for patterns. Go through your pins and categorize them. Once you feel comfortable with the categories, ask yourself, "Is this really me?" If not, cut! Be ruthless. Pare it down to 10 or fewer pins in each category.

PERSONAL BRANDING D.I.Y.

EXERCISE 7: WHO'S YOUR AUDIENCE?
Examine your dream customers to find your branding sweet spot.

Think about the people who hire you. Do you know who they are? When you're telling your brand story, knowing your audience is just as important as knowing yourself. If you don't know who these people are, it's important to get to know them now — who they are, how they think, what they wear, what they eat, where they hang out, how they like to spend a Saturday night.

I'm not suggesting you become a stalker, but the world is transparent now and you can research them on google. You can follow them on LinkedIn or Twitter. Take an interest and research their wins. The more you know about the people you're selling to, the more you can envision them, the stronger your brand will be. Because your brand is a bridge that will connect you to them.

GO!

Think of one person you're selling yourself to and write a paragraph or a page describing them in great detail.

REFLECT!

Study and analyze your description. What does it say about who you are and what makes you unique? Write your answer to that question in your Brand Journal.

PERSONAL BRANDING D.I.Y.

EXERCISE 8:
WRITE YOUR BRAND STORY

If you've made it this far, you probably are starting to have a pretty strong sense of your personal brand — the colors, qualities, attitudes, talents, imperfections, and quirks that make you the one and only you. Now it's time to synthesize all of that and take a stab at writing your brand story, which will become the core of your branded bio.

There was a time when I would encourage voice actors to write a professional "Who's Who, What's What" bio that read like a resume. But over the years, I've grown to value the power of narrative storytelling as a tool for showcasing your brand over those more traditional just-the-facts forms.

Helping my clients write their brand story is now one of my favorite activities because using storytelling rather than a dry resume allows you to share your authentic self in a deeper way that's relevant and intriguing to your ideal customer.

As you write it, keep in mind that the point is to woo your buyer, intrigue them, fascinate them, make them want to hire you. This is not your autobiography but a one-page enticement that conveys what it's going to be like to work with you.

Another way to think about branding is that it's all about flirting with your ideal customer, wooing them into taking the leap to hire you or audition you or sign you or whatever it is you want them to do to make your career bigger and more awesome.

GO!

Think about that person who you would most like to hire you — your ideal customer from the previous exercise. Now use the following tips to write your story (no more than one page total) in a way that conveys who you are while enticing that buyer:

1 In no longer than two paragraphs explain why you are uniquely the one to solve their problem.

2 Incorporate language you identified in previous exercises that most resonates with you.

3 Include one or two intriguing "on brand" facts about yourself such as you have a pet armadillo or you're a skydiver or a great cook or an avid gardener.

REFLECT!

Study and analyze your brand story. Does it feel 100 percent true? How could you make it stronger? Print it out and mark it up. Highlight your favorite parts.

DEMOS   LYNN NORRIS · TOUGH LOVELY VO   ABOUT   CONTACT

LYNN NORRIS

Tough Lovely VO

BOSSY FRIENDLINESS. YOUTHFUL RESONANCE.

Talent: Lynn Norris

Tagline: "Tough Lovely VO. Bossy friendliness. Youthful resonance."

What she's like: Lynn is as self-assured as they come and that's her appeal. She's tough yet feminine, and intimidating but in a good way. People want to listen to her.

Concept: I was in a branding workshop with Lynn and it instantly was apparent to me that she was bossy in the loveliest of ways and that's how she attracts her tribe.

Result: Doing a feminine twist on boxing gloves captured Lynn's essence and drew more people to her.

What she says: "The best part of launching my new brand is the consistent response of 'I love it!' that I've received from agents, potential clients and others in the industry. It fits me like a glove!"

CHAPTER 6:

BUILDING YOUR BRAND

Celebritize yourself one simple step at a time

Imagine that you wake up and go to your website. You look at it. You feel completely proud, effective and self-expressed. Your demos, your business cards, your auditions — everything is in alignment. It all fits together. It's all so completely you. It feels effortless, like it was meant to be. That feeling is Brand Nirvana, and it can be yours.

You've done a lot of hard work to get in touch with your brand essence. Now it's time to create the vehicles that will carry your brand out into the world. Do it right and you will achieve Brand Nirvana. There are several legs on this journey, and you're already part of the way there:

1 Get a Brand Journal and a Brand Buddy, complete the Brand Finder and gather testimonials. (Check!)

2 Study and analyze the Brand Finder, your demos, your testimonials and all other relevant materials. Then write your brand description and tagline.

3 Write a creative brief that provides direction on visuals, fonts, colors and so on.

4	Design your website and collateral.
5	Write your branded bio and any other remaining copy needed for your website and business collateral.
6	Launch your brand and your website and spread your brand story.

As a voiceover talent, you have the good fortune of actually being your product. This means that once you get your brand right, you will not only find success in voiceover but in every aspect of your life — a double-whammy of awesomeness. Complete the six legs on the journey to Brand Nirvana and you will find yourself in that magical place of alignment where everything feels right and true. I'm living proof of it.

Shortly after I launched my business, I was walking down the street when I noticed a handmade neon sign above a corner store. The little store had gone out of business, but the sign jumped out at me. I immediately felt a kinship with the shape of the letters. The font was hip and edgy and organic and well curated and artist-made. It represented somebody who wasn't afraid to express their opinion or be different. It belonged to somebody who saw the future. It spoke to me, and I knew right then and there that my business logo needed to have a similar vibe.

I hired a design team and told them what I wanted. They showed me some beautiful logo options, but none of them were quite right. They used existing fonts that came close, but that jumping-up-and-down feeling wasn't happening. I felt less connected to these shiny new logos containing my name than I had to that grocery-store sign — because it was one-of-a-kind. I realized I needed a one-of-a-kind font to represent my business, too.

I hired a graphic artist I admired to create a custom logo using a custom font. I had already done the initial work of branding, so I was able to give the artist a creative brief containing my brand description and tagline as well as visual direction. With everything so well thought out, she got it immediately. Et voila!: Celia Siegel Management - Branding, Marketing + Management for Voice Actors logo was born.

All these years later, I still feel happy every morning when I log in and see my logo. It's on my website, in my email signature, and on my business cards. It still feels like me. It puts a smile on my face and makes me want to go to work. And I still feel proud passing out my card. In fact, it does such a good job of conveying who I am and what I do that I've had people call me specifically to wonder aloud about how much I match my logo. Imagine that!

When you get your brand and your branding materials right, you feel better — and you do better. Not that getting it right is easy. To do so, you need to start by doing the brutal task of taking stock of everything you're currently doing. You need to be painfully honest with yourself about how it's working — or more likely not working — for you.

Pull together everything you are using to promote your voiceover career. All your demos (from your website, from rosters, from your agent's website and so on) and all your collateral materials (postcards, business cards, swag, website, etc). Then go through every single element one at a time and ask yourself the following questions:

- Does it capture your brand essence?
- Is it worthy of you?
- Does it (to borrow a phrase from decluttering guru Marie Kondo) spark joy?

Are your current business materials on brand? In most cases, you'll see room for improvement. Chances are, you are looking at a disorganized hodgepodge of styles and messages. Maybe there are a few salvageable items. But more than likely it's time to start over and build your brand block by block — starting with your domain name.

If there's one thing Twiggy, Morrissey, Adele, Fabio, Sting, Madonna, Liberace, Bono, Bjork, Cher, Prince, Eminem, Shakira, Farrah, Ice Cube and

Pink have taught us it is the power of making a name for yourself. You may not have been christened with a memorable moniker a la Beyoncé, but even if you are No. 14 in a long line of John Smiths, it's important to stake your claim to your name and start acting like people are googling you, seeking you out, wanting to know more about you, taking interest in your story.

Talent: Amanda Utter

Tagline: "Fetchingly fresh. Utterly authentic."

What she's like: Amanda is known for the delightful personality and charming spunk she brings to her performances, and she's based in Austin, Texas.

Concept: She's a voice talent and her name is Utter — we ran with the obvious word play — and layered those words over visuals that convey her hip Austin flavor.

Result: Her brand gets her noticed.

What she says: "Having a brand that captured my work and my personality gave me confidence that I could be as professional as I wanted to be. My website and tagline get me noticed and producers and talent agents comment on it. A lot of people have a good voice and demos and a website. Having this brand gives me an edge in a very competitive field."

To make sure your current and future fans find you when they google, you need to own your domain name. So right now, before you do anything else, if you don't own it already, go to a domain name registrar (the one I use is godaddy.com but there are zillions of them) and, for a small fee, become the master of your domain name. Depending on what's available, your preference and how common your name is, you want to take control of either yourfullname.com or yourfullnamevo.com. This should only take a few minutes.

This is the most basic step in making sure your website is search engine optimized, meaning when people search for you online, your site pops up at the top of the list. Another step toward SEO efficacy — and good branding —is to make your email yourname@yourdomainname.com. Or as Gerald Griffith of Voiceovercity puts it: "If you're using Gmail or another provider's email address for your business, you're building their brand, not yours." Make sure to check this task off your list as you build your website. More about later.

Once you have your domain name secured, it's time to take all the work you did in Chapter 5 and boil it down like a fine reduction sauce. The key to creating a DIY brand is simplicity. You can always layer on more elements (like a sub-tagline) later, but right now your job is to get to the essence. Think in terms of what sets you apart as you continue on your path to Brand Nirvana. Why are you different? What do you believe in? What is your passion?

While you are doing this intense work, it's important to keep your Brand Buddy and other supportive people in your life close. Despite my wholehearted love for branding, even I need support whenever I work on my own brand. As you move through this journey, you're going to feel vulnerable. You're going to feel conflicted. You're going to need a sounding board. That's just a normal part of the process.

This is a good time to warn your Brand Buddy that you're going to be high maintenance for a while, and schedule a few meetings. Once you've wrapped your head (and your Brand Buddy) around that idea, the next step is to start sifting through all the work you've done thus far and pull out the one feeling, the one written concept and the one visual that most speaks to and describes you.

How can you pick just one when there are so many awesome things about you and so many things you love? It's tough. But discipline is crucial at this critical phase in forming your brand. Your job now is to pick out the biggest and brightest stars. These three items will be the filters you use to come up with your tagline and your visuals. Take your time and choose carefully but don't overthink. You need to feel these choices in your gut. And try to have fun. When you have the right picks, you'll know it. It will just feel right. If it doesn't, journal about it, and start again.

But how do you know when you've gotten it right? When I work with clients, I see it in them — there's an adrenaline rush, followed by whooping and jumping up-and-down. I know this sounds corny, but I see it nearly 100 percent of the time. Even one client who is super low-key and never yelled woo-hoo confessed to me that she was so overwhelmed when she got her brand right that she almost screamed when she saw it.

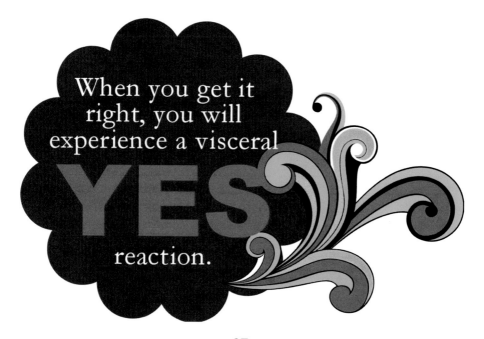

When you get it right, you will experience a visceral YES reaction.

There are several litmus tests you can use to make sure your brand is solid. The first one — and this is very important — is: Do you like it? Your brand should inspire you. It should be something that makes you happy to show up for work every day and to put yourself out there. It should help give you the confidence you need to share your voice with people.

You may be tempted to show your brand to your parents and your siblings and your college buddies and ask them to tear it apart. While a little 360 feedback can be helpful, having too many cooks in the kitchen is dangerous — especially cooks who don't know a thing about the voiceover industry. It's best to ignore these well-meaning folks. Do you feel calm and peaceful and excited about it? If yes, then you're good.

If you're not feeling it in your bones, look at the work you've done, think about yourself and your voiceover career, sort through it, and ask yourself how it makes you feel? If you feel like you're putting on a façade, it needs more work. If this is the case, there's a strong likelihood that your brand is too beige. You're playing it too safe.

● ● ●

Talent: Andie Duncan

Tagline: "Motherload VO. Where smart, serious and silly play extremely well together.

What she's like: Andie is a humor writer and an actress and a mother and a wife.

Concept: We put all of Andie's diverse qualities in our Brand Blender, and out came a visually sassy brand that captures her playful approach to being a wife and mother.

Result: By owning who she is, Andie increased her business.

What she says: "Since I launched my new site, clients will often say, 'We really like the approach you did on that such and such spot.' Hallelujah! Not only did they visit my site, but they actually left the homepage, played some demos and watched the videos (site stats don't lie)! My site is a virtual storefront that feels authentically me, and I'm incredibly proud of it."

Not only do you need to like it but also your target audience needs to resonate with it. By now you have done the research and thinking around that sweet spot between what you love and what the person you want to work for loves. That is your brand sweet spot. Have you arrived there? If not, you need to go back and do a little bit more work.

Once you have made your selections, the next step is writing your tagline — a pithy, catchy phrase that captures your essence and communicates volumes about you. You should now have a clear idea of what your brand is. This step is all about communicating that to the world. The goal is to say as much as possible about you in as few words as possible.

Think about shopping at Target. Think about all the words that you could use to describe Target. There are hundreds of options and yet Target has chosen one simple phrase — Expect More, Pay Less — that the company repeats over and over again. It captures the essence of Target and it speaks volumes about what it's like to shop in their stores.

Like Target, you have to pick one thing and you're going to say it over and over again. It has to be razor sharp, laser-focused, boom — the essence of you.

Look through all the material you created in Chapter 5. There's a chance your tagline is already in there somewhere, fully formed, a perfect phrase you can pluck out. Or maybe there's something close that just needs a little massaging to perfect it.

Sometimes ideas come easily. Sometimes you can play with a cliche. My former client Elizabeth Hales is so obviously shiny and charming in everything she reads that we played with an old cliche when creating her brand. Elizabeth really is the apple of your ear. "The Apple of Your Ear and Apple Head pic have been working for me for 5 years now," she says. "Clients remember me as the girl with the apple. I feel because I have strong branding, I'm able to work full time as a profitable voice actor."

If it's not, no worries. Just start playing with the one written concept you chose in the previous step along with words, phrases, and ideas from those Chapter 5 exercises, riffing. Invite your Brand Buddy and/or other wordsmithy friends to play with you. Think of it like a game of beach volleyball. Bumping, setting and spiking ideas around until you score.

elizabeth hales

voice over • the apple of your ear

demos • contact • blog • on-camera

When I get to this stage in the branding process the mental image that comes to mind is that of a blender. You take all those unique ingredients that make you a one-of-a-kind human, toss them in a Brand Blender and hit pulverize to see what comes out. Whatever it is needs to be a mixture that is yours and yours alone — a DNA strand that succinctly captures your dark side and your bright side. Often it's the blending of opposites — the sweet and the sour — that makes the recipe work.

When you get stuck, try playing with opposites. Are you casual or super buttoned up? Are you a hipster or formal? Using opposites can get your creative juices flowing and suddenly the opposite leads you to a riff in the right direction. Are you old-school or new school? How about no school at all? Or maybe homeschool, club school, coffee shop school, the school of rock, the school of hard knocks, the school of grit? Sometimes going to the opposite extreme of who you are can unlock a thought and leads you right where you need to be.

And if you are really stumped, consider hiring a professional writer to do the wordsmithing for you. (Or, in rare cases, you may decide, to heck with it, you don't need a tagline at all — you're going to let the visuals do the talking for you.)

ian McMullin

in{tell}igent^{VO}

putting the *art* in sm*art*

Talent: Ian McMullin

Tagline: Intelligent VO. Putting the *art* in sm*art*.

What he's like: Ian has 20 years of corporate finance experience. He's a CPA with an MBA who understands math, medicine and science. He also has a musically trained ear and a penchant for character voices.

Concept: Thanks to his unique background, Ian has a knack for delivering technical, sophisticated, academically dense scripts with ease. His delightful arts-math combo appeals to clientele who want a "smart" sound. His brand describes both Ian and his ideal customer.

What he says: "Intelligent.VO fits me like a perfectly tailored suit. The brand connects authentically with who I am as an artist and as a person and helps set the client's expectations of what I do best in the booth. This brand really positioned me to powerfully own my niche in the marketplace."

Kelley Huston Voiceover

demos   clients   reviews   studio   contact   about   news

- COMMERCIAL
- NARRATION
- INDUSTRIAL
- E-LEARNING
- PROMO
- VIDEO GAME
- ANIMATION
- TELEPHONY

social

what FRIENDLY sounds like

what SPORTY sounds like

what CATTY sounds like

what SMART sounds like

what LOVE sounds like

what REAL sounds like

what a DEMON PRINCESS sounds like

Talent: Kelley Huston

Tagline: None

What she's like: Kelley Huston is a jack-of-all-trades who does a wide variety of work. Her personality is vibrant and a bit quirky.

Concept: Being a jack-of-all-trades does not make for a strong brand in itself, so we created a bunch of mini-brands to accentuate all the work that she is hired to do in a fun way that shows off her many talents. Playing off the look of celebrity magazines, we formatted the design layouts to look editorial and slightly sensationalized.

Result: Producer Cliff Zellman told me that this was one of the favorite actor websites he has ever seen: "Sometimes I'll see a website or logo design and think, 'Wow! that's really terrific.' Then a few seconds later I'll think, 'Dammit, why didn't I think of that?' That's exactly what I thought the first time I saw Kelley Huston's website. So original, so engaging and so..... why didn't I think of that? It tells her complete story all on one beautiful, humorous and extremely well laid out page that's as fresh as the day it was made."

What she says: "My clients are creatives working in all realms of advertising and entertainment. They appreciate brands that are conceptually and visually interesting. I know this because they often make specific remarks, ask questions and compliment me on my website. The biggest and most pleasant surprise about my branding has been that it's an excellent conversation starter. It's been an opportunity to connect and build relationships in a natural way."

Once you have a tagline that's right for you, you'll know — it will fit you like a bespoke garment. You'll want to repeat it again and again.

The next question is: What's the right color palette for you? It's probably staring at you from that Pinterest board you created in Chapter 5 — or the single image you chose as your filter. Your job right now is to select one color that's you. This color will form the basis of the color palette you use on your website, in your signature and so on.

Before you settle on a color scheme, do a little research to make sure the colors you choose don't date you. Perhaps you love the mauve and teal hues of the '80s because you associate them with happy memories. That may be your color comfort zone, but those aren't the colors you want to use to brand yourself. Think of it like that favorite threadbare sweatshirt you wear around the house — or the stuffed animal you kept from childhood. Are those the first things you want people to notice about you? Nope.

Before you lock in, go to pantone.com and read about their colors of the year for the past several years. Then look at that visual you chose in the previous step and really look at the colors. There are probably dozens of colors in that image. As you make your selection, consider that colors have meanings:

- Green is the color of progressiveness, the environment, money and what's next.
- Blue is the color of business. It sends a signal of trustworthiness, calm and security. (I often suggest this blue for voiceover clients who do narration and corporate work — to show they are serious and professional.)
- Red is spicy, risky, bold — the color of passion and danger.
- Yellow is cheerful, optimistic, youthful and confident.
- Orange is exciting while exuding energy and warmth — and a sign of high creativity.
- Purple is the color of beauty, wisdom, spirituality, and science-fiction.

- Pink is the domain of the feminine and girly.

- **Black is serious and luxurious.**

- White is eye-catching, clean and simple.

Where does your brand fit into this color wheel of successful corporate brands?

While you're at it, play with your name. Is your first name also a color? I'm talking to you, Scarlett, Hunter, Violet, Kelly, and Rose. How about your last name? That's right Mr. Black and Ms. Green. Using the associations already built into your name can be an effective mnemonic device. But only if it's a natural fit that conveys something about your brand. You want any word play to be clever, easy and sophisticated, not corny. If you get stumped, consider hiring a designer who will work with you on developing a color palette that expresses your brand.

Dean White

Where appealing confidence and engaging
enthusiasm meet for happy hour.

Just as colors have meanings, so do fonts. It's fascinating to me how the shape of letters can tell a whole story. Because I'm a brand geek, I pay a lot of attention to how the stories of the fonts I encounter speak to me as I go about my day — tales of comedy, drama, romance, corporate intrigue. And I cringe when I see a font that doesn't match up with the brand message.

Since doing that font exercise in Chapter 5, I bet you're more tuned in to the fonts around you, too. If you want to geek out — and learn — more, I recommend watching the documentary Helvetica, which dives into the history and psychology of this ubiquitous font. It's a crash course on the impact a font can have, and a truly engrossing film that will get you in a new font state of mind.

As I mentioned, I used a custom font for my logo — and if you want to hire an artist to create a font for you, go for it. But I don't recommend custom fonts for every client. In this digital age, there are so many amazing fonts out there that if you don't have something in mind, you can shop around and find one that speaks to you.

Look at your Pinterest board of fonts and think about the message these fonts send. Are they clean and businesslike, clean and futuristic? Are they edgy? Artistic? Dynamic? Play around here and let yourself make your own opinion about what these fonts are saying. Now compare what's there to brands you're attracted to. Big brands put millions into choosing the right font, so you might as well take a page from their playbooks.

As you narrow down your font preferences, consider these rules of thumb for choosing a font that matches your brand.

1 The first rule of choosing your font is this: Don't use Comic Sans! It's the font everyone loves to hate.

2 Serif fonts, which have little extensions adorning each letter, are serious, traditional and official. Elegant even. The font equivalent of dressing up in a well-made suit. If you do corporate narration or do voice work for law firms or banks, a serious serif might be right for you. This is not the font category for someone with a very character-y voice. This is the category for voices of authority.

3 Sans serif fonts, which lack the serif adornment, are modern, streamlined and clean. I pair the san serif font — Helvetica — with my custom logo font in all my materials. There it is on the cover of this book: Helvetica all the way!

4 Script fonts mimic handwriting — and like each person's own script vary widely. They can be fun and casual. They can be formal and elegant. Pulled together, glamorous, classic, elegant, feminine, womanly, polite. The list goes on. That's one reason script fonts are so popular. You can easily make a logo by simply writing your name in a script font that's on brand for you. And while you can have a script font made from your own handwriting, ask yourself if your actual handwriting looks like the brand you're trying to express. Chances are, it won't.

5 Decorative fonts are attention grabbers. And they should be used sparingly. If you choose a decorative font, use it to make your statement and then switch to something simpler for your message. My custom logo is a decorative font. I'd give everyone a headache if I wrote all of the copy on my website in that font. Helvetica is a nice neutral secondary font that is also on brand for me.

Keeping all this in mind, go to fonts.com, and start typing your name into the fonts that match your brand. When you find one that feels right — 100 percent right — that's your font. If you're struggling, don't settle. I can't emphasize enough how important font selection is — your font sets the tone for your brand so choose carefully. If needed, hire a pro designer at this critical stage.

Once you have your font and tagline in place, you can begin to build your website. Choosing a main image is the next order of business.

What's the secret to choosing your main website image? If you have it in your budget, and it's on brand for you, an editorial-style custom photo shoot can give you wonderful results.

These voice actors successfully use editorial photos of themselves to showcase their personalities. It works for them because their brands, lifestyles, and personas are in perfect alignment.

If a photo shoot is not on brand for you or in your budget, all you need is one high-quality stock image that captures the essence of you. Stocksy, Istock, take your pick. There are so many great stock photo sites! The only hard part is choosing. But before you go hunting, a word of warning. Not all image sites are created equal: Some are much more expensive than others.

Take Sally Clausen. She has a remarkably vast voice. She's a former dancer and she's very womanly and sassy. She's also a real go-getter. Normally I curate images for my clients, but Sally decided, "I'm going to go out and look for female fabulous pictures."

Shortly thereafter, she came to me and said, "I found the picture. It's perfect. I love it. Quit looking — I found the picture." Nobody ever says that to me. I got the picture. And I loved it! Then I noticed the source. It wasn't a stock image — and it was expensive — $3,500 for one usage for three years.

I told her, "No, no. You have to get stock photos — royalty-free. We can spend $12 to $15 at Stocksy on a quality image that will be just as good for your brand." But she was attached and it really was perfect. I negotiated the price down to $1,800 and we kept it. Her thinking was, "This is going to springboard me and I feel so good about it."

Sally Clawson

Remarkably Vast Voice. Unheard of Female Fabulousness.

| Demos | Resume | Contact |

| On Camera | Speech Coach | Teacher |

Sally was happy with her image and decided it was worth it. But I've had other clients become fixated on an image that is just plain off-brand. Whether you're spending $12 or $3,500 an off-brand image is a waste of money. As the saying goes, a picture is worth a thousand words. Those words need to be 100 percent on brand. You are choosing an image you will see every day as you do business and is out in the world telling a story about you. You have to love it.

You have to feel at ease with it.

Go back to your tagline, your color, your word and your Pinterest board. Then start searching stocksy.com (or another good stock photography source) for an image that aligns perfectly with the other elements you've already created or selected. Dismiss any image that isn't a perfect fit, until you find the one that is 100 percent you. That's your image. And again, I can't say it enough, there's no shame in seeking professional help from an experienced designer.

Once you have tagline, font and image in place, it's time to build your website. And just to be clear, this is not about building any old beautiful website. You can have a beautiful, functional, SEO-optimized website that stinks. I see it all the time. Voiceover talent websites that look good at first glance and are ineffective because they have no personality — no brand. It pains me to think about the money, time and effort wasted by these artists on websites that lack branding, because they just don't work.

If you're doing it yourself, I suggest a one-page, endless-scroll website, the simpler the better. Use a website builder such as Squarespace, which makes it possible for non-techie non-designers to build a website. Still, the process is more complicated than, say, setting up a Facebook profile. Be sure to allow yourself plenty of time and expect some hiccups along the way. And again, seek advice as needed.

Also: Be warned that it will likely take a day or so for your finished site to populate on the Internet. But it will be worth the wait when at last you unveil your brand — your new celebritized self — to the world. Ta-da!

● ● ●

Talent: Alan Adelberg

Tagline: "Boyish good sounds. Modern man appeal."

What he's like: Alan is a smart, cool, youthful guy.

Concept: We positioned Alan for his demographic as a young, smart, modern guy.

Result: His brand helps him stand out from the sea of guys next door. The image of the cool, casual guy riding his bike over a bridge captures his essence and conveys his sound.

What he says: "Celia perfectly summarized my particular brand in a way that makes me stand out from the crowd. Potential clients looking for my vocal type instantly know they've come to the right place as soon as they see my landing page and read the tagline. Before I had my brand, my booking rate was influenced primarily by the number of auditions I could complete. Since launching the new site and brand, the amount of direct work I receive from site visitors alone is staggering. They all compliment the aesthetic and volunteer that once they saw my site they knew they were working with a professional. Working with Celia didn't just define my career, it skyrocketed it."

CHAPTER 7:

IMPLEMENTING YOUR BRAND

Countdown to launch

Recently I needed business cards and I was in a hurry. I usually go with a higher-end printer, but this time I thought, "What the heck? I'm in a hurry. I'll just Google a cheap printer.

I got the cards in the mail and they were perfectly OK. Just fine. I opened the package and found a flimsy box with an ugly label. The cards themselves were nothing special. But whatever — the information was accurate. I went off and ran my life.

Soon, I had to order another set of cards. This time I used MOO custom printers. When the MOO package arrived, it was a delight to open. The cards were beautifully printed. They came in sturdy, pretty boxes. They came with a note written in a clever, conversational way that made me chuckle. The cards themselves were amazingly smooth — they felt great in my hand. I could not wait to hand them out. I went off and ran my life, but this time I felt fabulous every time I reached for one of my cards.

You, my friend, are like those business cards. You are the product. How do you want to be packaged? How do you want your customers to experience you? Do you want to be perfectly OK? Just fine? And completely forgettable? Or do you want to be memorable, delightful and leave them wanting more?

310 • 621 • #### | Rebecca@RebeccaDavisVO.com

f y ⏷ in G+ ⏷

HOME   DEMOS   CLIENTS   **REBECCA DAVIS**   KUDOS   BLOG   CONTACT

listen ▶ _____ 00:00 ⏷

Rebecca Davis is a Voiceover Actor known for her versatility & range.

Rebecca brings an abundance of training and experience as an actor to every voiceover project. She began her professional stage career in New York at the ripe old age of six, and has been performing and entertaining audiences with her sugary charm ever since. She currently resides in Los Angeles, where she earned her MFA in Acting from UCLA, and is a long standing Resident Artist of the critically acclaimed theater company, Moving Arts.

commercial demo ⏷

Talent: Rebecca Davis

Tagline: "Sassafrass VO. Sugary Charm. Wicked Versatility."

What she's like: She's versatile and sassy.

Concept: When I presented the idea of Sassafrass to Rebecca, she said, "OMG! That's what my husband calls me!" Bingo! It's a word that has attitude but can be sweet or spicy.

Result: Rebecca specializes in character work and this brand quickly showcases her versatility as an actor.

What she says: "After my brand launched, the number one thing that surprised me was how much my confidence rose. I felt like I had a whole package that I could proudly present to anyone without hesitation. And it worked. People have told me how impressed they are, how memorable my brand is and that it really matches my personality — especially my business cards."

In this business, you don't have a choice, of course. Your voiceover success hinges on being the latter. That's why you've spent so much time honing your talent. That's why you embarked on this personal branding journey. And that's why it's so important to filter all your collateral, all your communications and every business decision you make from here on out through your brand.

Having a basic branded website is a huge step in the right direction! But you're not done. Just because you've built a website doesn't mean they'll come. You need to put that brand to work for you by putting it out into the world in a consistent, strategic, business-minded way. A brand is only as strong as the people who know it.

Now that you have your tagline, your visual brand identity, and your website, the next step is to create your business collateral. When I work with clients, we recommend creating five pieces of collateral, and I suggest you do the same. They are:

1 E-signature

2 Business cards

3 Social media banners

4 Postcards or fold-over thank-you cards

5 Branded stickers

I'll walk you through how to do each of these shortly, but first, for your brand to take hold, the question "Is this on brand?" needs to become your mantra. Your look, your color palette, your tone, your font, your message, your essence — everything has to match in order to avoid brand confusion and brand diffusion. The way to ensure this is to create brand rules that will help you answer these questions.

Before you start creating any collateral, you'll want to make a list of these rules — a style guide — and put it someplace for easy reference. This style guide will be your key for every visual and communication decision you make.

It will keep you on track when, say, you find yourself drawn to a fabulous fuchsia color while reprinting your business cards. Or veering toward a delicate new font. Or itching to wear a dangerous-looking leather jacket in your new headshot. Are those choices on brand? Do you see fuchsia in your color palette? Is delicate on message? Is being dangerous part of your essence? When in doubt, consult the style guide. If it doesn't fit, don't do it.

Use these rules consistently, and everything you send out will be cohesive — a seamless extension of that brand you worked so hard to build. Achieving Brand Nirvana isn't enough — you need to stay there, living in that space, to reap the benefits for the long term.

You'll need an e-signature that includes your contact information and tagline as well as a link to your website. A branded e-signature is a simple way to constantly market yourself. Every email you sign will not only reinforce your brand and make it easy for people to reach you but also encourage recipients to check out your website and listen to your demos. Use your signature on every email because you never know where it may travel. Maybe somebody that you email about a personal matter knows somebody who hires voiceover and — bingo! — a connection is made. Plus, it just makes you look like a pro.

You'll also need business cards. I adore business cards — I love to line up all of the branded business cards I have created for clients. It's like a little art museum, with each card telling the story of its owner. But branded business cards are more than eye candy — they are a powerful marketing tool especially when used as part of a personal interaction.

My clients frequently recount stories about the confidence they feel with a branded business card in their hand. Holding a card they're proud of gives them a kick in the pants to reach out to someone they might have shied away from in the past. That's why, once they have their branded business cards in hand, I challenge them to hand out 250 business cards in the next 12 months. I challenge you to do the same. Just think about what making 250 little personal connections could do for your career — especially when you're leaving your brand behind each time.

Those business cards will be working for you long after you've left the meeting. Likewise, you can — and should — use social media to make your brand work for you while you sleep, work and otherwise go about your days. Make sure your LinkedIn page matches your website which matches your Twitter page. Coordinate your social media banners so that anytime anyone glimpses your online presence, they think, "Oh, there is that awesome voice talent again!" It may seem boring to you, but most people aren't engaging with your online presence day in and day out. Your No. 1 branding goal is to educate the world about your voice. Consistency is an absolute must.

Kelley Huston Voiceover

what REAL
sounds like

cell: (512) 964-3447
info@kelleyhuston.com
www.kelleyhuston.com

THE SOUND SOLUTION
KEVIN DALY VO.
SOLID DISTINCTIVE AND HANDSOMELY ORIGINAL

Cards are also a great tool for connecting and reinforcing your brand. Getting a card in the mail is a delightful surprise these days, which is why I encourage my clients to be generous in sending out branded postcards or fold-over cards. These cards should be simple and low-key — not overtly self-promotional. Use them often — to thank a new buyer, to thank an agent for a meeting or for a fab booking, or to congratulate somebody on a promotion or an award. You can't send too many personal cards.

Lynda Robertson
Just like a Woman VO
Sassy sophistication & supple wisdom
custom mingled to make you look good

LYSSA
GRAHAM
PANTS ON FIRE VO
WWW.LYSSAGRAHAM.COM
LYSSA@LYSSAGRAHAM.COM
PHONE: 409-939-1251

Likewise, branded stickers are great because they're so versatile. You can slap them on anything from your outgoing business mail to a potted plant. And you can turn literally anything into swag with a sticker — Hula-Hoops (I actually did that once), water bottles, notebooks, bottles of wine, kegs of beer, or a gorgeous box of cupcakes or doughnuts (guaranteed to make you the darling of the office coffee break). You could even place a vinyl branded sticker on your skis or snowboard — you never know when an opportunity might arise to connect with a voiceover buyer. You could be riding a chairlift with one and, bam, there is your sticker on the tip of your board to help spark that conversation. And if humor is in your brand you can have a little extra fun by creating funny on brand messages on stickers.

If you really want to kick it up a notch, you can also create branded swag. The trick with swag is creating something that is both on brand for you and a nice little gift to your customer. Have you ever had the experience of being at a conference and standing right next to the garbage can with your swag bag tossing out the junky stuff? You don't want to be the person sending out stuff that goes directly in the trash. Before you put your name on something, ask yourself: is your brand a 50-cent trinket from China? But that doesn't mean you need to spend a lot of money either.

The best swag is useful — a high-quality pen or pencil, a journal or notebook, or a gift card. As with the thank-you cards, you want to keep the branding subtle. You don't want make your logo so hard-core front and center that your clients won't use it. The goal here is fond brand remembrance. Give your clients something they want to use, and when they do, they will think fondly of you. Over the years, I have collected lots of swag from talent. The items that were nice enough to hang onto include: cute coffee cups, water bottles, phone wallets, quality notebooks, pens and pencils, highlighters, coolers and picnic blankets.

Don't leave them with feelings of guilt and shame for filling a landfill with another piece of useless junk. Don't give anything branded as a birthday or holiday gift. And if you don't have anything nice to give, don't give anything at all. Good swag is thoughtful, creative and filtered through your personal brand — a little leave-behind that reminds others of the unique authentic wonderfulness of you.

Once you're all geared up and ready to go, you'll probably feel like shouting it from the mountaintops. But hold your horses for a sec, sisters and misters. While you do want to exude your brand everywhere you go in every situation, being scattershot in your business efforts isn't going to get you the voiceover career you deserve. You need to be intentional about who you reach out to, about the work you want to book, about creating relationships and so on. In other words, with every decision you make from here on out, you need to ask yourself: Is it on brand?

Of course, to pay the bills you likely will take voiceover work that is not necessarily in your favorite genre, but it's important to consistently focus on the career you want to have — to constantly be going for it, intentional with branding and marketing, intentional with building relationships and intentional about your social media targets. If you just want to do animation, you're going to have a different path than someone who wants to focus on audiobooks. The same applies to e-learning, promo, affiliate, automotive, corporate narration, long-form narration, gaming, telephony, radio imaging and so on. Or maybe, like many talent, it's not about genre for you — you are open to bringing your unique specialty to all the wonderful voiceover genres out there. These are important considerations as you take the final step before launch and make a business plan to implement your brand.

I'm one of those people who always has an up-to-date 30/60/90-day plan, a one-year plan, a three-year plan, a five-year plan and a life plan that I am working. I geek out on business planning as much as I do on branding. That's because business planning is the yin to the yang that is branding.

Most of my clients — shockingly — do not share this passion. I would say a good 75 percent of the actors I work with want to vomit when I tell them what I am about to tell you: You absolutely have to have a business plan.

Mary Ellen Lord, Voice Agent Department Director at SBV Talent, says branding and business thinking are the factors that set successful talent apart. "All things equal in the performance area (listens, takes direction, can replicate performance), it will be a talent's personality and demeanor that will separate them from the pack," Lord says. "That, and having a grasp on the fact that this is a business."

But before you reach for Pepto-Bismol, take a deep breath while I talk you off the ledge.

Your business plan is simply a statement of where you are now and where you want to be in a certain time frame. It's like a map with an arrow on it leading from Point A to Point B. Being mindful of where you are and where you are going — and then breaking that down into actionable steps — will help you zero in on your target audience and decide exactly how to market yourself. Like having a brand, having a business plan makes everything else you do easier.

This sheer act of claiming what it is that you want and envisioning yourself obtaining it can be a powerful force in propelling you toward your goals. Like a pro athlete visualizing herself scoring the winning point, you need to get in the zone. A business plan will get you in the zone so you can score in the bloodsport that is the competitive world of voiceover.

Because so many of you are clutching your Pepto-Bismol, I'll keep it simple. This powerful 3-step business plan is an abridged version of the one I use with my clients.

1 Write down exactly where you are in your voiceover career today by answering these questions:

- How many auditions are you getting?
- How much money are you earning?
- What agents are representing you? And how are those relationships going?
- What is your booking ratio? (Use this number x average price per booking to reverse engineer how many auditions a day you need to do to meet your financial goal. For example, if you average $500 per job and want to make $500 per day and your booking ratio is 1 in 20 you need to read 20 auditions a day.)
- Do you use pay-to-plays? If so, analyze your profiles for optimization.
- Define your target markets. What are your niches and/or market segmentations (Promo, Commercial, Radio Imaging, Narration, Animation, Interactive & Games, Audio Books, etc.): How have you pursued, landed and/or maintained work in your niche market/genres up to this point?
- How has your business grown in the last year?
- What has worked for you? What do you regret not doing?

2 **Where would you like to be one year from today? Write down your goals.**

- Include what genres you would like to pursue, what products you want to be working on. Be as specific and detailed as possible.
- Include training and personal goals. Who do you want to study with? Who do you want on your team? List these people.
- How much money do you want to make each month?
- In your experience, what are 10 things you can do to determine your own success?
- In what ways could you accelerate your business now to reach that goal?

3 **Create small actionable steps toward reaching each of these goals. Put these in your planner. And have your Branding Buddy hold you accountable.** (Fun fact: The simple act of writing these things down makes it 41 percent more likely that you will achieve them.)

CHAPTER 8:

SHARING YOUR BRAND

Make your brand work for you online, offline, all the time

Are you ready to educate the world about your voice? You have all the tools in place — it's time to launch!

By now you should be feeling excited about taking full control of your talent and your career. You are armed with everything you need. You own your brand and you have the tools to put it out there. You're no longer at the mercy of anybody else. You no longer will be spending your limited time seeking approval.

Instead, as CEO and brand ambassador for your voiceover business, you will spend your time educating people about your awesomeness, upping your skills and managing your brand. There are only 24 hours in a day and you are not going to waste any of them by going all beige trying to please someone else. You are a strong brand and strong brands don't please everyone — what they do is attract their tribe.

You need to let the buyers and agents know about your talents and skill sets. And a big part of your job is to embody the identity of your voiceover business in appearance, tone, message, and vibe and to actively manage your personal branding strategy. That means it's up to you to remind people that you exist.

You've got your product — you! You've got your brand — yay! You've got your swag — nice work! Now you need to plug it all into the machinery of self-promotion. It's time to connect, connect, connect — and to truly enjoy rocking your talent in the coolest industry on the planet.

One of the most important things you can do in your business — and your life — is to build and nurture relationships.

Have you ever heard someone's voice and felt an instant connection? Like love at first listen? Like they were speaking right to you? What I'm describing is a voice crush.

When a buyer or agent hears you for the first time, and gets those butterflies in the stomach, they will instantly want to know more about you. You can leave them high and dry, or you can give them everything they need to take the relationship to the next level.

But relationships don't just happen. They require intention and attention. Now it's up to you to use your personal brand not only to attract attention but to turn these voice crushes into full-on, major love affairs.

> **To build solid VO relationships, you need to do three things:**
>
> **1** Make a marketing list.
>
> **2** Reach out and attract attention.
>
> **3** Stay in touch and keep things interesting.

Your marketing list should include not only those who have hired you but also those who almost hired you and those who might want to hire you. These are the people you're going to educate about your brand. These are the people with whom you're going to build relationships.

If your list is small right now, that's OK. You're going to start building it today through social media and in-person meetings. You're going to grow this list fast by setting (and following through on) two challenges.

> **Challenge 1:**
> Add five names a day to your marketing list. That may sound like a lot at first, but when you have the whole Twitterverse plus Google and LinkedIn at your disposal, it's not so hard.

> **Challenge 2:**
> Give away one entire box of business cards —that's 250 cards — each year.

As you add names to your marketing list, you will follow the same brand launch steps — the same enticements — for each of them. I perform five steps with every brand I launch. They are proven to attract attention and help you stay on message. As you complete each step, remember to ask yourself: "Is it on brand?"

Step 1:
Branded Bio

When I work with clients, as soon as the brand is done we write a branded bio. This is not a resume — it is a one-page aspirational, magnetic, vibrant proclamation of who you are, your biggest talent and what you are passionate about in the world.

Your branded bio will become the basis for your social media bios and any other bio you need to write. It needs to be short, authentic, on brand and written in the third person. This super powerful statement of awesomeness will form the basis of all your interactions.

Branded bios give you an opportunity to enhance your brand story and add more detail about how your brand will benefit the buyer. A good branded bio also improves your SEO as does any on-brand written content. It is your business proof and like everything else, must be on brand.

Start with the rough bio you wrote while completing the Brand Finder exercise as well as the Brand Story you wrote from chapter 5. Then infuse your bio with your brand. Include your tagline and other language from your Brand Journal that served to help you uncover your brand. Then remove anything that's off-brand, especially any long tangents.

Then write a headline for your brand — it can be longer than a title and should convey your brand. For example, the headline for my client's brand Supernatural VO: "Her name is Julie Shields, and Legend has it that her voice powers are supernatural ….". Sometimes my clients have a hard time "bragging" about themselves. When in doubt, ask your Brand Buddy — or hire a professional writer.

All the Moms, All the Moods, and All the Professionalism a Client and Piece of Copy Could Ever Hope For …

Andie Duncan is an accomplished voice actor – and, you guessed it, a real-life mom, too – whose broad ranging vocal performances have appeared on radio, film and television. She made the leap to voiceovers in 2010 after two decades as a singer-songwriter and performer, which saw her open for artists including Joe Cocker, k.d. Lang and Sarah McLachlan's Lilith Fair, just to name-drop a few.

Andie's JUNO and VAA Nominated voice has reached audiences worldwide for companies including Airmiles, Acura, Arby's, A&W, Arla … and that's just the A-list from her motherload of great clients!

Beyond all her supermom, free-range mom, mommy dearest, sancti-mommy, soccer mom, helicopter mom, tiger/pick your animal mom, and who-knows-what-they'll-call-the-next-mom vocal insight, Andie has the natural facility to communicate with optimum impact, articulating your brand message from authoritative to warm and reassuring, or from the playfully comedic to the downright sultry read.

Hey, and if that's not enough, she's loads of fun, faster and more efficient than a mom rockin' carpool, school conferences, a work deadline, Costco trip or a baby & me yoga class – all before lunch. And she can take and follow your direction before you get the chance to tell her that there's some puke she may have missed on her shirt.

From the ISO booth in her professional midtown studio, Andie can connect to clients and be directed via Skype, Source Connect and ISDN … or tin cans and string if you want to kick it old school. So, go take the VO load off your back with Andie today – and don't forget to call your mother!

● ● ●

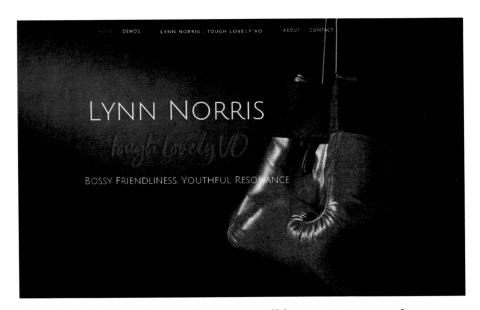

Lynn Norris' knock-out talent can pull in, protect, or push your audience around with a friendliness so spry they'll think they asked for it and then ask for more.

Tack on the ease and speed with which she delivers, and it's no wonder she's fast becoming a leading female contender in the highly competitive VO ring.

Lynn's got a full locker of vocal aptitudes & attitudes that can resonate with big brains, tender hearts, smart asses, silly gooses - and your toughest customers therein. Her opera background and love of animation gives her an extra appreciation for the dramatic and the ridiculous.

After a long career in financial software development, Lynn is also fluent in "tech speak", "financial copy", "software education", "compliance concepts", and she knows how important it is to deliver your information in an easy to digest and engaging manner.

Experience what it sounds like to win, and let Lynn's Tough Lovely VO get scrappy with your script today!

Step 2:
Branded E-card

Create a beautiful, concise branded e-card. You can create a general message, and send it out to your entire list, or a genre-specific e-card that is targeted to a particular industry, such as automotive, animation or political. The card should contain your name, your tagline, a call-to-action line linking to your website/demos and your contact info. Maybe even include a testimonial. This is an introduction — an announcement to the world of the awesomeness that is the authentic you.

Think of each card you send as a seed you are planting. Sprinkle these seeds widely and with joy. Don't expect an immediate result. You never know when one will sprout.

Step 3:
Branded Social Media

Social media is where things really start to get exciting. Rather than solely interacting with your predetermined and set marketing list, social media allows you to get on the radar of people whom you would not otherwise have access to:

- That casting director from Disney? She's on Twitter!
- The leading recruiter for Zappos? Connect with him on LinkedIn.
- Your next client? Sure they are on social media, do a little searching and see what you can find out about them!

Your presence across the various social media channels acts as a box of virtual business cards inserting themselves into the memories of potential clients, friends and other connections. If you have a sloppy looking Facebook page — eek! — that's no better than a crumpled up business card. And if you're not active on any social media networks, that's worse than having no business card at a networking event.

And just as business cards need to have a certain amount of information, it's absolutely crucial for you to ensure that all of your social media accounts include the following:

- Bio
- Tagline
- Headshot
- Branded banner

Talent: Jillian Nielsen

Tagline: "Well Said Jillian. Playfully Smart Talent"

What she's like: On top of being an amazing talent, Jillian nails it every time because she is so thorough and businesslike and detail oriented.

Concept: Her work is always on point, never sloppy. Every word is well said.

Result: This brand gives Jillian the confidence to work shoulder to shoulder with corporate clients as a trusted business equal.

What she says: "The most surprising change I've seen since launching my brand is the level of confidence I have when presenting myself to potential clients. I feel like I have always had confidence in my abilities, but now I'm able to convey that more readily to everyone else!"

If you don't have a professional headshot that shows your personality and professionalism and exudes your brand, it's time to book a shoot. In the olden, golden days of voiceover, we agent-types tried to keep the talent's face out of it. We wanted clients to hear with their ears, not their eyes. But in today's marketplace, it's impossible to keep anyone's face under wraps — the best you can do is control your online persona.

That means having a great headshot and using it consistently. Although you won't ever lead with this image, you will use the same headshot image across all social media platforms and you'll want to make sure your hair, makeup, and wardrobe are on brand without being over the top. A selfie won't cut it.

Before diving into the various social media networks and specific tips and tricks, I'd like to mention one thing. Do not feel the need to be part of each and every network. I am not saying that you cannot, but if you choose to have one of each social media network out there, make sure you are doing it consistently and beautifully.

Too many times, I come across social media networks that were created and then abandoned. For example: The last post was from November 2010 and it says "Hi, I've joined Twitter!" Rather than spread yourself too thin, choose one or two social media networks and do them well. Once you have one off the ground you can always expand and add another. And I recommend starting with Twitter.

Many people in the voiceover industry are hanging out on Twitter — and for good reason. Twitter allows you to get on the radar of people to whom you would not otherwise have access. You can use Twitter to build community, find your tribe and reach your ideal customer. Another plus: Twitter moves fast and has a short memory. So if something you do doesn't gain traction, you can try something else. No need to dwell on it.

When you set up your Twitter account (or rebrand the one you already have), be sure to include the following: A headshot, a bio, and a branded banner. Upload that on brand professional headshot. Your Twitter bio will play a big role in helping others decide whether to follow you. Include your tagline, your location and your website here. Upload a banner image that shows off your brand — I suggest using your website image if possible. Then it's time to start tweeting.

Not sure what to tweet? Remember that this is social media — the whole point is to interact with others. And, as in any social interaction, being gracious and generous goes a long way. Entice others to follow you by sharing what you know ("Follow me if you want to know about _____."). Get people to tweet back by sharing on-brand compliments ("I loved your take on _____."). Ask what people want, how you can help them. Ask engaging questions to encourage conversation such as "If you were stranded on a deserted island and could only have 3 things, what would they be?"

Once you have the hang of it, develop a hashtag for something you have expertise in. For example, whenever I post a handy tip, I use #CSMtip across my tweets. This helps my followers find my advice in search.

LinkedIn should also be a high priority for building your voiceover business. It is the only social media network designed for making professional connections. Tracy Lindley has found voiceover success by leveraging this powerful tool.

"One of the first pieces of advice I got from a successful entrepreneur specializing in social media marketing was to join LinkedIn," writes Lindley on her blog.

"I really had no clue why I should hop aboard yet another social media train at the time, but I did it. I took a selfie, loaded up some info about my professional life, typed up a quick bio and that was that. Cross another one off the list. I truly did nothing with said profile for months.

"Then one day, I got bored and started clicking through some of my

LinkedIn contacts. Mostly other voice actors, a few friends, and that was about it. I suddenly noticed that there was a drop-down menu to the side of the search box and decided to see what my options might be. The more I played around with the many features of LinkedIn, I slowly realized that this had become my new favorite social media platform, as well as a window of opportunity.

"I now use LinkedIn daily to not only meet the right people, but gain new clients, book voiceover jobs, and develop mutually beneficial business relationships."

Remember that five-contacts-a-day challenge? LinkedIn is the fastest way to grow your marketing list. It worked for Lindley, and it can work for you.

When you set up your LinkedIn account you'll want to follow similar steps as you did for Twitter. Use your professional headshot. Create a vanity LinkedIn URL that contains your name. For example, www.linkedin.com/in/celiasiegel. Your LinkedIn profile is an online resume. Ensure that your profile is complete. Use the "projects" section to link directly to your demos. Add skills and get endorsements, which are easy-peasy one-click acknowledgements from your network showing that you are recognized for a specific skill. Edit your headline to be descriptive or it will automatically appear as your current or last position held.

Facebook tends to be more personal, and many of my clients prefer to keep it that way — a private friends-and-family space where they can share pics of kids, pets and celebrations. Others find it to be a natural extension of their brand.

Many Facebook experts will tell you to have a separate business page for your business. I used to subscribe to that — until I really thought about it. Sure, I understand the need for companies and those who aren't forward facing in their business to have one. But for voiceover talent, it's different because you are your voice and you are your business. Unless you have frequent Facebook interactions that are off-brand, you can maximize the power of your personal Facebook profile by showing your true authentic branded self there — in a more casual environment. And if you're going to use it for business, be sure it's branded with the professional headshot, banner, bio and so on.

You've already gotten your feet wet by using Pinterest as a tool to finding your brand essence. If you're enjoying it, keep it going. I love Pinterest and use it in my business to curate brands I like as well as in branding my clients so it's an invaluable tool for me. And it's easy to create private boards where you can pin items of personal interest, like kid birthday party ideas, that may not be on brand.

Instagram is a 100 percent image-based platform so while it works for me since visual branding is a huge part of what I do, it may not be the place for you to strut your brand. But if you have a knack for visual storytelling that would be a boon to your brand, make your profile public. Choose an Instagram handle that's consistent with your name and all of your other business social media channels. For example, I've claimed @celiasiegelmanagement. Use the Instagram bio for your tagline and a link to your site.

What to post? A picture from your latest audition, a quote image related to voiceover on a nicely branded background tagged with your handle, a 30-second video that shows a behind-the-scenes peek at your recording setup.

Whichever social media networks you choose to utilize for your business, it's important to be intentional about using it. Develop a strategy, decide on a schedule and be consistent. Don't start going to town on Twitter with 20 tweets in one day and then not tweeting again until the next election. People want to come to you for valuable information. If you are sharing it inconsistently, people won't see you as a thought leader or expert in your niche.

Decluttering queen Marie Kondo says the secret to eliminating stuff you no longer need is to pick up each object and ask yourself, "Does this spark joy?" If it doesn't spark joy, you should get rid of it. It's such a simple, almost laughable idea, but it's brilliant. I've really incorporated it into my life and business, and I believe it even applies to your social media efforts. Your social media presence should spark joy!

Kondo says you have to hold something in your hand because you actually have to experience it. Same goes for social media. You have to experience each platform and its capabilities so you can decide how to make it work for you. Confusion and frustration don't spark joy, so sometimes, this means learning how to use these platforms. (The more you educate yourself, the more fun it gets!)

Give each platform a chance. Learn how to use each one. Then ask yourself: Was it fun? Did it allow me to express myself and be authentic? Did it fit with my personality? Did I kick up my heels and get a bunch of retweets, or did it distract me?

I recommend Twitter and LinkedIn because they have the most business utility, but if you love Facebook or Instagram instead. Then go for it. Give it your heart. As long as you're doing one platform really well (with joy and authenticity), you can make things happen for your business and your brand.

Whatever platform (or platforms) you choose, pay attention to your written voice. As with every other aspect of your brand, your writing needs to be consistent and distinctively on brand. Do you have a wicked sense of humor? An air of almost-overconfident grandeur? A casual way about you? Then be sure to write your posts that way.

Twitter at first did not spark joy for me. I was afraid I'd say the wrong thing. Once I realized that Twitter is just like being at a cocktail party — where you don't need to calculate every word that comes out of your mouth — it became a lot more fun.

This doesn't mean I'm giving you permission to banish everything in your life that doesn't spark joy. Meeting with my accountant doesn't exactly spark joy right away … but the finished report of my yearly finances … that certainly does. Sometimes in life and business, the joy comes at the end.

It's your job to make sure people know who you are. That is on you — not your agent, not the buyer. It's your job to connect, to use social media to your advantage. Show off. Help people. Spread your passion. Above all, be real, be on brand and be ready to be amazed.

Step 4:
Branded Newsletters

Create a regular branded newsletter. Think of this monthly missive as a newsie letter to your marketing list. Keep it short. Keep it simple. Keep it upbeat. And use this trick to get people to click: Make it more about the readers' needs than your own. What does your audience want? What interests them? What would make their lives easier?

Step 5:
Branded Networking

Remember my challenge to hand out your whole box of business cards in the next 12 months (tick-tock!). Well, if you're going to do that you'd better get out of the booth and do some good old-fashioned face-to-face in-person networking! You've got your elevator speech. (Right? If not, grab your Brand Buddy for an elevator speech role-playing sesh). You've got your business cards. You've certainly got a little of that I-am-who-I-am swagger. It's time to take it all on the road.

Make a plan to get face-to-face at least once a month. Attend a Chamber of Commerce business event. Go to a convention where the buyers are and make an effort to meet them. Register for a conference. Buy that new

LinkedIn connection a coffee. Request an informational interview. Go to a Meetup. Remember to balance meeting peers (which is important) with meeting those who can hire you. But resist the impulse to schmooze only with your peers. It might be uncomfortable at times, but it will be worth it.

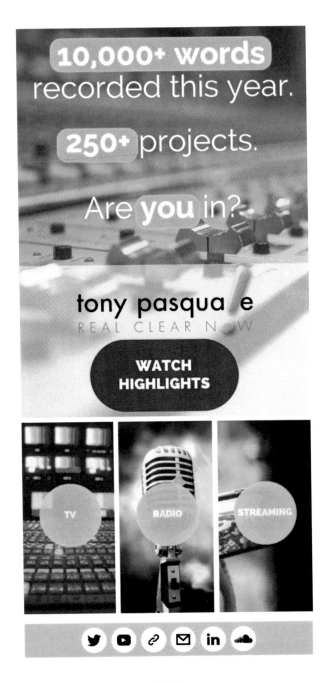

NOT LIKE THE OTHER.
GOOD BRANDING IS IN THE DETAILS. SEE HOW THESE 3 MEN DIFFERENTIATE THEMSELVES.

Building relationships is a lifelong endeavor, and to do it effectively you need to be armed with your branded business cards and your elevator speech. You need to be brave. And you need to be persistent.

It takes many many touches before any consumer chooses to make a purchasing decision. And while you definitely want to avoid being an annoying high-pressure salesperson, I'm here to tell you that most people give up way too early. Most people start to internalize not hearing back — not getting a yes —and they quit trying. Business connections are lost to the timid.

For many of my clients, this aspect of being a VO CEO is difficult. But that doesn't mean it's impossible. Anyone can cultivate a positive sales mindset — and the truth is you have no choice. The talented salespeople do one thing that sets them apart from the easily discouraged: They see each new connection as just one on a never ending list. Their catchphrase is, "Next!"

There's an old adage in sales that says it takes many noes to get a yes. When you have a sales mindset, the word "no" becomes a reason for excitement — a sign that you're one connection closer to a yes.

Marketing is a numbers game — just like your booking ratio. How many auditions do you need to do before you book one? How many people do you need to educate about your brand before you get noticed? Know these ratios and you're less likely to be discouraged. When you've got the talent — and a great brand — the rest is simply a volume game — you just need to put your voice and your brand out there enough times to have a successful career.

And then, when you do get a yes, nurture it!

That's the reason you have those branded thank you cards. You truly can't send too many thank you cards — unless you send the same exact card to the same exact person.

Keeping track of everyone on your ever-growing marketing list can be a challenge. It's important to keep meticulous notes documenting who you talked to, when you talked to them, what you talked to them about and then set reminders to follow up. You can do this using a journal and a paper calendar, a spreadsheet and your digital calendar or a customer relationship management (CRM) app to manage this. The important thing is that you do it.

It's also important to respond to tweets, share interesting articles on LinkedIn and reach out promptly to new connections. Your job is to do the stuff you love; be who are you; and share it on social media, on your website, and in person. The point is to let people into your world by using the power of marketing and social media to show them who you are.

You may even want to take it to the next level and become a thought leader in your particular niche by creating a professional blog.

"One of the things that surprised me the most about branding in general is that clients actually pay attention," says Joe Zieja, LA based voice actor.

"Because the flow of work can be so fast and furious, I often don't think that clients have the time or the desire to actually look and see who I am and what I've done. The small details of my career and my life couldn't possibly be important to someone I've never seen face-to-face. But it is!" Joe says. "I'm always surprised when a client emails me and says that they've seen something else that I've done, or takes the time to write after reading a newsletter to congratulate me about something that's been going on in my life."

If the idea of writing a newsletter or blogging —or any of the above — is too daunting or simply just not your thing, don't fret. Remember to keep that magic trick of delegating up your sleeve. You are the CEO of your business and great CEOs are masters of delegation. There's no shame in hiring people to help you.

If you want to blog, but you're not a great writer, you can still have a blog. Just hire a ghostwriter who can interview you and then translate your ideas into blog form.

The key is being as intentional about your time and your money as you have been in creating your brand. If you're spending so much time cleaning your house that you never find time to build your marketing list, then hiring a housekeeper for a few hours each month is likely money well spent. You only have so many hours, you only have so many skills. No one can do it all. Successful people know this and have the confidence to seek help when needed.

How will you know if your VO brand is working? Go back to your business plan and look at your goals. Are you getting measurably closer? Is your bottom line rising? Are you getting more auditions? More agents? Better agents? Better relationships with the agents you have?

You've embarked on a lifelong endeavor. You will never be finished. You've just begun planting the seeds that will lead to an outward growth spiral. Your focus will forever be on honing your brand and making it more valuable and visible.

Once you get started you'll notice ripple effects and you'll become more effective at capitalizing on them. When someone pays you a compliment via email, you'll thank them, then follow up to ask them if you can use it as a testimonial on your website, then post it on your website and include it in your newsletter. One thing will lead to another. And you'll soon discover that your brand will take on a life of its own. Those business cards, that website and everything else you put out in the world will be working for you even when you're sleeping. When your brand is always on, you don't have to be.

● ● ●

Home Demos Videos About Clients Contact Blog

Holly Franklin

Hollypop VO!

Satisfy your sweet tooth and make your copy **pop**!

Talent: Holly Franklin

Tagline: "Hollypop VO. Satisfy your sweet tooth and make your copy pop."

What she's like: Sweet as candy, sweet as pie, sweet as they come, sweet like sugar. Did I mention sweet?

Concept: Listen to Holly's demo at her website while looking at her brand. Need I say more?

Result: This brand infuses trust by matching up visually what we hear. If you want a sweet charming voice, Holly Franklin's your gal.

What she says: "I'm 97 percent sure Celia Siegel is secretly a mind reader. She dove into my brain and created a brand that makes me feel like I'm on a freakin' Disney World vacation every day of my life! Not only did I score the best brand ever, I've also gained confidence in business strategy, marketing, and VO performance! Here's a lil' proof in the pudding: I just booked an exciting animation gig, a preschool series, and a videogame! She chop, chopped my Hollypop into spunki-licious action!"

CHAPTER 9:

A BRAND NEW WORLD

Watch everything in your life get better

Once you have your brand, you will notice things starting to fall into place. Truly. I know it because I live by own advice. I also hear it again and again from my clients. And I never tire of it, of the joy and wonder and sheer confidence that emanates from people who have figured out how to share their authentic true self with the world. I love seeing my clients jump up and down. I love watching them achieve financial success they never thought possible. I love hearing about how branding manifests itself in their lives in unexpected ways.

One of my clients blogged about the effect her brand had on her. "Somewhere deep in my psyche a light bulb went off and things started to change," wrote Lyssa Graham in a July 2017 post. "All of a sudden, I was completely happy with my very own self. And that light bulb illuminated every aspect of my life.

"Seriously, for the first time in ages, I love my hair. I figured out what clothing styles look good on me and now that's what I wear. I am ridiculously comfortable in my own skin. No more trying to fit my square peg into anyone else's round holes.

"Actors are adaptable. That's what we do. We play the roles that our audiences want to see. We have to. Otherwise, we're just really funny waiters. But sometimes all of that adapting can cause us to forget who we really are. We're just too busy being what others want, to remember what we want to be."

Once you have your brand and get it out there it becomes one of your most cherished assets. But it's important to remember that while you created it, you don't own it. One of my mentors growing up was my French teacher. She told me that all I would ever truly own is what was between my ears. Your brand will go out into the world and take on a life of its own. Soon it will start doing work for you like a little elf cleaning your house while you sleep. That's also another reason to make sure it inspires you and truly reflects you.

● ● ●

home   about   videos   resume   contact

Julie Shields's brand is SuperNatural VO. Her tagline reads: " In your backyard believable. Out of this world fantastic." And this is what she says about it: "It's not so much a change as it is a confidence that I have knowing that I'm putting my best foot forward and am presenting myself in a way that I know represents me and my voice accurately and in a fun way."

You should be feeling some of the positive effects by now. Walking a little taller, feeling a little more comfortable in your skin, more money in your bank account.

A strong personal brand creates passion and possibilities. It helps you see the path of success before you and how to remove any obstacles — internal or external — that may be in your way. Thinking about yourself as a brand will give you confidence.

At its heart, branding is about being authentic and living in the moment and connecting. When the brand is right, when the branded demos kick ass, when you feel powerful and confident, there will be a true snowball effect. Work begets work. Confidence builds confidence. You put your brand out there, and you get one agent and then another agent. You book a job, which gives you another experience to talk about on social media and in your blog, and then you get another job. Instead of being a lump of snow that can't get out of the starting gate, you become a happy little snowball racing down the hill gaining size and momentum as you go.

What you've done so far is amazing. You've created a brand that is so you. Now it's time to start living it.

Once you start presenting your brand with 100 percent confidence everywhere you go, once you start putting yourself out there day in and day out, once you truly commit to showing up today and every day looking successful and being successful by being 100 percent you, 100 percent on brand, you will reap the rewards.

When my clients do this, the benefits are unmistakable.

"I always have a zillion projects going on in a zillion different disciplines - voiceovers, music, story slamming, composing, clowning, writing, hosting," says Nina Rolle. Her brand, "Truth Be Told VO. Because there's always more to the story," telegraphs her multifaceted career.

"Celia has helped me to weave all these together into one cohesive brand that positions me to be competitive in the VO business, without amputating all the other interesting projects that make up my artistic life," she says. "The most surprising change I've experienced is a shift of framework: I have gained a new perspective on my own story, my own personal brand. I am operating at a much higher frequency and looking at life through the eyes of a successful person. Consequently, I have more ownership of my career and more confidence in who I am and what I have to offer, both as an artist and a voice-for-hire. Something got shaken loose working with Celia. I'm way more focused, way more tapped into my power, and having way more fun."

Nina Rolle
TRUTH BE TOLD VO

because there's always more to the story

This is what living your brand feels like.

Are you ready for doors — the right doors — to open? Are you ready to walk through them with confidence? Are you ready to find your tribe? Are you ready to have the success that can only come from being your one true wonderful self?

You have done the hard work of branding. Now it's time to feel the magic — the newfound self-assurance that comes when you make your authenticity obvious to the rest of the world. The heightened confidence every talent experiences when they get their brand right. The swagger that comes from living your truth. The success that comes from being a Voiceover Achiever.

● ● ●

You have your brand, but this is only the beginning. Now it's time to live your brand, to inhabit it every day. Practicing these five habits daily will help keep your on track.

1 Commit to being on brand today.

Spend a few minutes today using your brand as a filter to see what is out of alignment and off-message in your life. Do you need more exercise? A tweak to your elevator speech? A different hairstyle? A different studio setup? Get out your Brand Journal and write it down. Then set a realistic goal and list action steps for how you're going to make the change. Put these action steps on your calendar.

2 **Talk yourself up today.**

Look at yourself in the mirror each morning and give yourself an out loud pep talk. Not sure what to say? Create a list of positive affirmations. You can find thousands of affirmations online. Choose a few confidence-boosters you need to hear, write them down, post them and repeat them often. For example: "I am a voiceover superstar." "I radiate confidence, certainty, and optimism." "I courageously open and move through every door of opportunity."

3 **Commit to taking care of your instrument today.**

Move your body, eat healthy foods and hydrate. When you take care of yourself, you'll have more energy to attract your tribe.

4 **Commit to educating five people about your voice today.**

Who are you going to educate about your voice today? Write them down and schedule a time in your day to reach out. These can be new people to add to your marketing list or people you need to follow up with. Just make sure it's five a day, every day.

5 **Commit to doing your daily auditions.**

Remember the booking ratio and minimum number of daily auditions you calculated back in Chapter 6? What's the number again? Make sure you're doing it every day.

ABOUT THE AUTHOR

Celia Siegel is the founder of Celia Siegel Management, widely recognized for building strong personal brands for voice talent. Before creating CSM, Celia was a respected talent agent with stints at CESD, JE and Wehmann. A brand builder, certified life and business coach, success strategist and talent manager, Celia has advanced the careers of top VO talent for more than two decades.

Working from the undeniable and exciting truth that great brands wield great power, Celia's multi-leveled expertise and extensive knowledge of the ever-changing voiceover industry has helped voice actors across the globe successfully brand and grow their VO businesses. In her first book, VoiceOverAchiever, she shares her winning formula for creating standout brands that ignite standout careers. Keep in touch and find out more here: CeliaSiegel.com.

CREDITS:

Edited by Heidi Raschke
Designed by Biondo Studio

BRAND JOURNAL

BRAND JOURNAL

BRAND JOURNAL

BRAND JOURNAL

BRAND JOURNAL

BRAND JOURNAL

BRAND JOURNAL

BRAND JOURNAL

BRAND JOURNAL

BRAND JOURNAL

BRAND JOURNAL

BRAND JOURNAL

27619689R00090

Made in the USA
Lexington, KY
02 January 2019